Job Search Mastery

How to WIN Your Dream Job

Job Search Mastery
How to WIN Your Dream Job

Tom Caravela

©2024 All Rights Reserved. No portion of this book may be reproduced, stored in a retrieval system, or transmitted in any form or by any means-electronic, mechanical, photocopy, recording, scanning, or other-except for brief quotations in critical reviews or articles without the prior permission of the author.

Published by Game Changer Publishing

Paperback ISBN: 978-1-963793-47-5
Hardcover ISBN: 978-1-963793-48-2
Digital ISBN: 978-1-963793-49-9

www.GameChangerPublishing.com

DEDICATION

This book is dedicated to EVERY job seeker that I have had the pleasure of speaking to and working with over the course of my professional career. YOU motivated me to write this book. The emotional journey of the job search process is not one that should be taken alone.

The challenges are real. The process can be intense. Thank you for the inspiration to make *Job Search Mastery* a reality. May the pages of this book provide the guidance, energy, and inspiration you need to WIN.

"If you are in a job transition, this is the book you have been searching for! Tom's experience and knowledge will motivate you to ultimately win your dream job. Regardless of industry, from entry-level to senior executives, this book was written for everyone and provides the right information at every step along the job search process."

-Jim Wilkinson, Ph.D., US Medical Leader, Argenx, and former VP, Medical Affairs, Amgen

"Tom Caravela is NOT the prototypical search firm owner; he is a servant leader and pioneer in the career development space. I have had the pleasure of witnessing the value he brings to his clients and candidates on a daily basis. It is nothing short of inspirational! If you are on the job market... you NEED to read this book."

-Aaron Opalewski, CEO and Founder, Spark Talent Acquisition

"Tom Caravela is the perfect blend of talent advisor, motivational coach, and job search virtuoso. He has deep, robust experience within the job search and talent acquisition arena. This is a must-read for anyone navigating their career journey."

-Jennifer Bookspan, CEO, Bookspan Search, and former CEO, Forbes.jobs

"Tom Caravela is not just a master of the job search; he's a relentless pioneer in the field. His passion for excellence and his commitment to sharpening his craft are truly inspiring. In his latest work, Tom distills his extensive experience into powerful, practical advice for job seekers everywhere. Having witnessed his profound impact on professional lives, I can attest that Tom's guidance is transformative. "Job Search Mastery" is an essential tool for anyone looking to navigate the complexities of the job market and win their dream job. Tom's dedication to helping others is unmatched, and with this book, he extends his reach even further, continuing to shape careers with unparalleled expertise. For those in search of meaningful career advancement, Tom is the job search guru."

-Donnie Gupton, Creator of the Relevant Recruiter Method, and Co-Founder, Ora Marketing

"Tom is a talent and job search master who understands exactly what top companies want and how job seekers should navigate the search process. This book is a must read for anyone in career transition."

-Gary Stauble, CEO and Founder, The Recruiting LAB

Job Search Mastery

How to WIN Your Dream Job

A Complete Step-by-Step Guide
to a Successful Job Search

Tom Caravela

www.GameChangerPublishing.com

Table of Contents

Introduction 1

Chapter 1 – Mindset for Job Search Success 5

Chapter 2 – What Is YOUR Dream Job? 15

Chapter 3 – Know the Target 25

Chapter 4 – Take Aim at the Target 33

Chapter 5 – LinkedIn: The Most Important Tool in the Shed 49

Chapter 6 – Job Search Process Roadmap 65

Chapter 7 – Networking: Building a Future for Success 75

Chapter 8 – Personal Branding, Social Media, and Engagement ... 89

Chapter 9 – The Interview: Planning and Practice 99

Chapter 10 – The Interview: Performance and Follow-up 113

Chapter 11 – Negotiate Your Way to Success 127

Chapter 12 – The System 143

Conclusion 149

Let's Stay Connected 151

Acknowledgments 153

Introduction

I believe in you, which may sound bold since I have never met many of you. But I know that you are capable of doing amazing things in your life and career. It doesn't matter how smart you are, how many years of education you've had, what degree you hold, or anything else. What matters are the actions you take, your commitment to your goal, and how consistently you decide to take those actions. Each day, you have a choice as to what progress you will make and how you will get closer to your dream job.

A recent report featured in *Inc.* magazine found that 73% of Americans think finding a job is one of life's most stressful experiences. Every day, people come to me looking for my help winning their next job: clients, friends, family, and complete strangers. Parents ask me to help their kids. "Tom, if you can just spare 15 minutes of your time, it will really help." Well, in reality, 15 minutes isn't going to help much at all.

So, I wanted to provide a resource where I can put all of my experience, knowledge, advice, tips, tricks, and best practices in one place to guide any and all job seekers. Look at this book as a series of private coaching sessions. Each chapter is its own session. Each session covers a critical job search topic and will lead you through the entire process one step at a time.

Step… by… step.

BUT TOM…

"I don't know where to start."

"I feel like I'm stuck."

"The job market is too competitive right now."

"How am I supposed to compete with people who have more experience than me?"

"I'm not sure what I want to do next in my career."

This is what I hear every single day. If this is you, you are in the right place. This book is for you. This system is for you. Throughout my 25-plus-year career, I have helped literally thousands of people win jobs with this exact process. I truly believe that the system is the solution. The system produces the outcome (in any area of life). Follow the right system, and you will influence your own outcomes. Learn this system, and you will have expert knowledge of the job search process.

You could be 16 years old or 60, a new recruiter, human resources professional, career coach, hiring manager, or just someone interested in learning the best advice on how to win a job. This book will guide you and give you the answers you need through a proven, step-by-step process. More importantly, after completing this book, you will have educated yourself on the exact system for any job search and will be equipped for the remainder of your career.

Now, forget everything you think you know about the job search process. The game has changed and continues to change. Depending on the study, "job application" success rates can range as low as 2% to 10%, which means the days of applying to a bunch of job postings and finding success are gone.

So, how are you going to find success in a competitive job market? How are you going to win your dream job? I WILL SHOW YOU!

To be clear, this book is a system. It's a process. It's not a quick fix, overnight solution, or the proverbial five-run home run. It's a series of singles, doubles, and triples that will help you win the game. The system I will outline in this book will not only teach you how to navigate a successful search process and win your dream job, it will show you how to develop the right career habits that will lead to great success.

What you will take away from this book will stay with you for your entire career, which is why I urge you to read these pages in order and in its entirety. The book's lessons build on one another in a specific order. If you go out of order, you might miss a critical step in the process. That said, you can always revisit chapters after the fact as a refresher for different stages in your search, but I do not advise reordering the steps.

Important Notes: First, expect me to use lots of quotes, stories, and teachings from the coaches, mentors, and leaders I respect and admire most. The greatest growth in my career came after committing to personal and professional growth through coaching programs, books, podcasts, and daily inspiration.

Second, I'm going to ask you to grab a notebook or purchase a journal to take notes in and use to complete the exercises throughout this book. The reason I would like everything in one place versus on a bunch of pieces of paper or sticky notes is so you can build on what you've done and keep it all together. This will be your **Job Search Journal**, which you can revisit throughout your career. Keep in mind that you may need to look for a job again in the future, and your job search journal will be a huge asset and a starting point for your next search.

One More Note: There are sections of this book that may appear to be for entry-level job seekers and not experienced professionals. I urge everyone to follow along, even if they have experience. The exercises all lead to a tactical application later in the book. At the very least, you will get useful self-inspection and learn from the assessments.

Now It's Time to Jump Into This Process!

Please remember—I am committed to your success. I believe in YOU and your ability to win your dream job. While you may feel alone at times, I will be here the entire way, rooting for you throughout the process. I invite you to commit to yourself and your future. The fact that you are reading this shows you are willing to take action. I encourage you to be thorough and fully vested in this process. I am grateful for your trust in me and promise to share every ounce of knowledge and experience to help you WIN.

I cannot wait to share in the celebration of your success!

CHAPTER 1

Mindset for Job Search Success

The very first place we need to start is in your mind. As with anything in life, mindset is key to your success. The best way to find success in your job search is to have the right attitude and mental game plan. During your search, you will experience ups and downs, challenges, and rejections. Having the right mindset and being prepared is paramount to the success of your search and will carry over into every area of your future career.

10 MINDSET PRINCIPLES FOR JOB SEARCH SUCCESS

1. No Shortcuts

It's very important throughout your job search process, and especially as you begin, to set realistic expectations that things will not happen overnight. There's no instant gratification, no workarounds. One of the greatest quotes I've heard in a long time was from entrepreneur, best-selling author, and investor Alex Hermosi, who said via LinkedIn, "The thing they don't tell you is, the long way is the shortcut because the shortcut never gets you there."

Let me share a story that I think really explains the exact mindset you need to have as you start your job search process. Charles Barkley is an NBA Hall of Famer. What's most significant is that he made it into the Hall of Fame without a championship ring. But when he first got into the league, he was overweight. His teammate Moses Malone was at the end of his career and became a mentor for Barkley.

One day, Barkley asked Malone, "Why am I not getting any playing time?"

Malone turned to him and said, "Because you are fat and lazy." Malone offered to help Barkley and said he needed to lose 10 pounds. According to CNN and ESPN interviews with Barkley, he went from around 300 pounds down to 290. At that point, Malone then said to Barkley, "Now I want you to lose another 10 pounds." So, Barkley lost another 10 pounds.

Well, this happened five or six times, and Barkley lost over 50 pounds. After all was said and done, Barkley asked Malone why he didn't just tell him to lose the 50 or 60 pounds right from the start.

Malone's reply was, "Because you may have never done it."

That's exactly how you have to look at your job search. You can't do it all at once. You can't expect it to happen overnight. You have to take your job search one day at a time, 10 pounds at a time. I will outline the daily and weekly action steps you need to take to achieve the progress you need to get you to your goal.

2. Progress Mindset

You will hear me talk a lot about the importance of progress. Many job seekers don't know where to start in their search, so they procrastinate. You cannot wait for things to be perfect. One of my favorite quotes from sales guru and motivational leader Zig Ziglar is: "You don't have to be great to start, but you have to start to be great." The idea here is to seek progress and not perfection. I will provide the roadmap in this book; the steps will be laid out for you. You just need to take action and seek progress.

One of the best ways to look at this is to follow the advice and research presented by Andrew Huberman, a noted neuroscientist and tenured professor in the Department of Neurobiology at the Stanford University School of Medicine. I recently heard him on an Ed Mylett podcast episode called "Unleash Your Brain Power and Growth Mindset." Huberman explained that dopamine, a hormone associated with pleasure and mood, is released anytime we are moving towards something and we think we are on the right path, not just when we actually get there and achieve our goal. So, dopamine actually rewards us for effort, progress, struggle, and the pursuit of our goals, as well as the anticipation of getting them.

Huberman says that the brain is always seeking novelty and reward. If we believe we are on the right path, we are rewarded with the release of dopamine. He says that we should be intentional about celebrating our efforts, progress, and struggles. So, keep in mind that throughout your job search process, focusing on progress will help motivate you and drive you to your goal.

3. Entitled to Nothing

I say this very respectfully and humbly, but you are not entitled to anything. It does not matter what degree you have, how many years of education, your experience level, who you know, etc. You must do the work. Success is earned. Success requires effort. If you're always expecting help or trying to find the path of least resistance, you will always lose out to someone willing to put in the extra effort.

Throughout my career, I have consistently seen senior-level job candidates get beat out by more junior candidates because they come into interviews thinking that they deserve the job just for showing up, while the junior-level candidates put in the time, preparation, and all it takes to win the job.

This reminds me of something I learned from one of my coaches, Ben Newman (one of the top five peak performance coaches in the world, according to *USA Today*). On Episode 16 of Andy Frisella's *Real AF Podcast*, Ben said, "Success requires grit. What is grit? It's a series of monotonous behaviors repeated over and over and over again. Every day… not just some days." Adopt the mentality that you can (and likely will) lose all momentum when you stop doing the work required to achieve success in your search and grow in your career.

4. It's a Competition

Your job search needs to be considered a contest because it is. You are competing against a pool of other candidates. No matter what job you apply for, there will be other candidates applying for the same position. As a matter of fact, if you apply for a position on LinkedIn, it will actually show you the number of other applicants.

Now, let me pause here and caution you not to get freaked out when you look at those numbers. There could be literally hundreds of other applicants for the same position you are vying for. Keep in mind, a good majority of those candidates are probably underqualified. To give you an example, I recently posted an executive-level position that required an advanced scientific degree, meaning a doctorate, and a minimum of 10 years of experience. In the pool of applicants, there was a barista from Starbucks with no degree and no professional experience. I actually thought it was a joke, but whether it was or wasn't, that was one of the candidates in the applicant pool. So, do not get freaked out by the number of applicants. However, it is healthy to look at your application as a contest. Imagine you are competing against someone who has either the same or more experience than you since that may likely be the case.

Here's a better way to look at it. I recently heard Tim Tebow on *The Ed Mylett Show* podcast talk about his motivation when he was growing up. He told Ed, the world's top performance coach, that he had a quote written on his wall that he would look at each day and say: "Somewhere, he is out there training while I am not, and when we meet, he will win." Someone else is out there preparing for the same interview. Someone else is out there getting references together. Someone else is out there networking and asking for job referrals to get in front of a hiring manager for the very same position. In the job market, someone has to win, and someone has to lose. Which one will YOU be?

5. Be Obsessed

You have to want the job badly. You must have a burning desire. You need to develop a sense of urgency that will drive you each and every day. If not, you will be beaten out by someone who wants the job more than you. One of the things I find myself saying to job seekers and even my own team is: "When all things are equal in a job search, the position is always awarded to the person who shows they want it the most." Hiring managers want people who are hungry for the job, who are running *to* something and not *from* something.

So, when I talk about being obsessed, it doesn't just mean that you really want the job badly. It means you have to be obsessed with your thoughts. You have to see yourself in the role. See yourself performing your dream job. If that means going to an office and performing certain tasks, visualize right now what it's going to feel like when you get to do that. Think about how much money you're going to make in that dream job. Imagine the feeling you're going to get when you see that money get directly deposited into your account. Think about how you're going to feel when you get to change your lifestyle because you just got to that new level of salary. This is what I mean by being obsessed. And the better you get at this, the closer you're going to be to winning your dream job.

6. Embrace Failure

One of the most difficult things for job seekers to imagine is the amount of failure and rejection they will experience. There is a well-known quote from the legendary author and leadership guru John Maxwell: "Fail early, fail often, but always fail forward." You may have heard this another way: "Fail fast and fail forward." Failing fast is an absolute requirement for job search success.

Please understand that rejection is a part of the job search. It's inevitable. It's not just you; it's everyone. It's just a part of the process.

Very early in my career, when I first started in sales, I had a manager named Steve Farrell. Steve said to me, "The sales process is like a deck of cards. There are 52 cards in every deck, but only four aces. So, sometimes, you have to turn over a lot of cards before you get to an ace. But just know, the more cards you turn over, the closer you are getting to your next ace."

That's exactly how you have to look at the job search. The aces are the job applications. The aces are the interviews. The aces are the job offers. Later in the book, I will outline very specific details about what job search activities you need to do. Those are the cards. The more you do these activities and the faster you do them, the closer you'll be to winning your dream job, the closer you'll be to turning over an ace.

But let me be clear: when I say to "embrace failure," I don't mean that we enjoy failure. I don't mean we should be happy with failure, and I don't mean we should chase failure. Instead, we chase progress, we chase success, and we move past our failures as quickly as possible.

7. The Rejection Pivot

How do you handle rejection? Embracing failure is a lot easier said than done. What do most people do after they receive bad news or experience rejection? They probably call their mom, dad, sister, brother, spouse, friend, cousin, aunt, someone/anyone and share in their misery. This could go on for hours. It could go on for days. It all depends on the person, but typically, people take a very long time to wallow in self-pity.

Here is how the rejection pivot works. After a failure, give yourself a few moments to recover – let's say 24 hours. After those 24 hours, when you get yourself back together, take positive action. Your response to the negative must be something positive. You need to counterbalance the negative and keep going. This is what it means to be unstoppable.

This is not natural. Typically, people will stop or pause at adversity and setbacks. If you can learn to pivot immediately after a rejection by taking positive action, you cannot be stopped. By the way, when you do this, others will notice. This is what we call true leadership. I credit this concept to another of my coaches: entrepreneur, best-selling author, and world-renowned speaker Andy Frisella.

8. We Win, or We Learn

Job searches have a lot of moving parts. If something doesn't go your way, the important thing to ask yourself is, "What did I learn? What can I take from this experience? What can I do better?"

Let me tell you the story of one of my recent candidates. Her name is Maria. The one thing that stands out about Maria is her tremendously vibrant smile. It's her signature. When she interviewed recently for her dream job, she made it to the final two candidates. Unfortunately, Maria was not selected.

She was devastated. When I saw her, her signature smile was gone, replaced by a look of despair, rejection, and misery.

I asked her if she had learned anything from the experience or gotten any feedback from the hiring team. Thankfully, she had. They told Maria that she'd done really well in the interview but came off as a little more nervous and with a little less confidence than the other candidate. Boom, there's the lesson.

So, Maria now knows what she needs to tweak for next time. She knows exactly what to practice and how to prepare for the next interview. There's the win. Turns out, Maria was actually called back to interview at that same company for another position. At the time of writing, we still do not know the outcome.

9. Focus on Process, NOT Outcome

It is very easy to get overwhelmed in your job search. As a matter of fact, you should expect it to happen. The job search process may take much longer than you expect. You may feel stuck and frustrated, like winning the job is never going to happen. Stay focused on the process. Don't look past it.

Let me share a quote from the book *The Boy, the Mole, the Fox and the Horse* by Charlie Mackesy. The boy is leading the horse through the woods and says, "I can't see my way through."

The horse says, "Can you see your next step?"

The boy replies, "Yes."

And the horse tells him, "Just take that."

That's how you need to look at the job search.

You can't look at the end result. You can't worry and say things like, "When am I going to get the job?" "Am I going to get the job?" or "How am I going to get the job?" Focus on the process, stop looking at the goal, and stop worrying about the outcome. Just worry about what's right in front of you. When you focus on the process, you make progress. When you succeed in your daily actions, the outcomes will take care of themselves.

10. Discipline (Consistency of Action)

The key to your job search success is discipline, which is the ability to consistently take daily action to implement the process. Commit to the daily actions that will inch you toward your goal. This is what I mean when I say "process." It's a daily routine that helps you build and build and build. Discipline is doing things automatically and consistently even when you don't feel like it. Success happens one day at a time. It's a game of inches. The inches will become feet, the feet will become yards, and the yards will turn into touchdowns.

You need to create your own momentum. You cannot wait for others to do it for you. When you are disciplined and consistent in your daily actions, you will create momentum. Momentum leads to confidence. Confidence leads to more action. More action leads to more momentum. That is how you WIN. This is what progress is all about. Quite simply, I am asking you to develop new daily habits that will lead to you winning your dream job and also carry over to your future career success.

I encourage you to come back and read this chapter again after you complete this book. These 10 mindset principles will become more evident and make even more sense during and even after your search. There may be times when you will need a reminder of how to think and what your mindset should be to lead you to success, so consider revisiting the principles, especially if you start a new job search in the future.

Chapter 1 Summary:

10 Mindset Principles for Job Search Success

- **No Shortcuts**
- **Progress Mindset**
- **Entitled to Nothing**
- **It's a Competition**
- **Be Obsessed**
- **Embrace Failure**
- **The Rejection Pivot**
- **We Win, or We Learn**
- **Focus on Process, NOT Outcome**
- **Discipline (Consistency of Action)**

Free Download: 10 Mindset Principles for Job Search Success Summary.

Scan the QR code:

CHAPTER 2

What Is YOUR Dream Job?

You MUST identify your target. Now that you have the right mindset and attitude, it's time to take the first step in the process. Before you start your search, you must have a very clear goal, a target. You need to be crystal clear on what you want. Whether you are an entry-level candidate or someone with 30 years of experience, clarity on what you want to do next in your career is extremely important. **What is your dream job?** The answer to that question sets the direction for the entire job search process.

Before we get into exactly how to do this, let me explain why it's so important. I'm going to use the explanation that I recently heard from renowned psychologist, author, and online educator Jordan Peterson on what it means to be aimless. Peterson says, "When you are aimless, it creates anxiety." He gives the example, "If you were dropped in the middle of the desert, you would be anxious. Not because you don't know where to go, you would be anxious because there are too many places to go."

When looking at our job search, it's very important to take aim, to have a goal, to have a target. So, how do we do that? This is a lot easier said than done, and it can be very difficult for certain people, especially those who have no idea what they want to do next in their careers. To make this as easy as possible, I've broken it down into a simple five-step process.

1. Vision

You need to begin with the end in mind. What is the vision for your life? It's important to complete a quick self-assessment, which I will help you do in this chapter. Please take out your job search journal so you can jot down your results after doing the next few exercises.

First, ask yourself these 10 questions. Try not to overthink them.

1. What is the vision for your life? What do you want?
2. Where do you want to live?
3. How much money do you want or need to make?
4. Do you want to work in an office, or do you prefer or need to be virtual?
5. Are you open to travel? Some positions require a certain amount of travel. What percentage are you willing to do?
6. How far of a commute will you consider? Keep in mind that one of the greatest stressors in any job is the commute.
7. What is your short-term career goal?
8. What are your long-term career goals? Where do you see yourself going?
9. What interests you the most?
10. When do you want to retire? Even if you are young, you still need to think about this question.

2. Personal Core Values

What do you value most? Core values are your deeply held beliefs and priorities. Why are core values important, and why do we need to know what they are? Identifying your core values will help to inform and guide you. Let your core values guide your thoughts, decisions, and actions to align your life path and career with what's important to you.

To give you an example, I'm going to share my seven core values with you:

1. **Faith**
2. **Family**
3. **Fitness/Health**
4. **Wealth/Prosperity**
5. **Excellence**
6. **Service**
7. **Peace**

I share my core values as an example, not to instill any of my beliefs in you or to try to convince you that these need to be your core values. I just want you to see an example of what it means to live by a set of values. When you start interviewing, it's going to be very important to see what the companies' core values are and if they align with yours.

It's very simple to find core values in most companies nowadays. They actually put them on their websites. Some companies exercise their core values more than others. Basically, the values define the culture of an organization, and you need to decide whether or not you want to be a part of that culture and if those core values will align with yours.

Please use your job search journal and make a list of your core values. The list should have from five to ten values. I wound up with seven just because that's what suited me. If you're having trouble, I have provided a downloadable list of 25 core values that will give you some guidance.

Free Download: List of 25 Common Personal Core Values.

Scan the QR code:

3. Strengths and Transferable Skills

Before I explain why it's so important to know what your strengths and transferable skills are, I want to tell you a story. A wealthy dad had a teenage son who was about to get his driver's license. The son asked his father to get him a new truck for his birthday. He wanted it to be black, a certain make and model. He was really excited about getting a new truck for his special day.

Well, on his birthday, the father grabbed his son and walked him out to the garage. The boy stood there, excited to see his new truck, but when the garage doors opened up, there was no truck. Instead, there was a lawnmower, a weed whacker, and some landscaping equipment. The son looked at his father with shock and disappointment and asked him what all this stuff was.

The dad explained, "This is *opportunity*. When you learn the skills that it takes to be successful and make your own money, you'll be able to buy as many trucks as you want. They could be black, they could be any make, any model, and you can buy as many as you want. But you have to learn the skills first."

The young man started mowing lawns in his neighborhood, and he earned enough money to buy his own truck. He eventually sold the landscaping business and later became a lawyer. He is now a very successful attorney and a wealthy dad.

Identifying your strengths and transferable skills is a very important part of this process. It will come up again in our work together later in this book.

To identify our strengths and transferable skills, you will need to do another quick self-assessment. Please take out your job search journal if you haven't already because I want you to ask yourself these questions. Again, don't overthink them.

1. What are you best at?
2. What is your special area of expertise?
3. What type of work brings you energy?
4. What are you passionate about?
5. What comes naturally to you?

Many strengths that come naturally are called "signature strengths," which are innate. Chances are we had these strengths when we were three, and we will have them when we're eighty-three.

To provide an example, I will share my personal strengths and transferable skills with you. When I was growing up, at a very young age, I started talking. I would talk to anyone and everyone, anytime, anywhere. I would hold full conversations at a very young age. People used to say, "Wow, this kid was born with the gift of gab." Basically, that was their way of saying I was a good communicator.

My signature strength is that I had strong interpersonal skills at a very young age. People would say, "You would make a great attorney or a great politician." Well, it turns out I became neither. But I did become a pretty darn good salesperson and executive recruiter, which then led me to own several businesses and become a keynote speaker, trainer, and coach. I also wound up with my own talk show, developing a successful podcast that has made it to the top 2% globally in the careers category rankings.

So, my "gift of gab" brought me to a place where I found my passions. Finding my passions resulted in success. More importantly, it brought me career satisfaction. What I do does not feel like work to me. Identifying your signature strengths and using them in your career is critical to your success and future job satisfaction.

4. Weaknesses and Developmental Areas

While we need to know what comes naturally to us and what we can leverage, we also need to know our weaknesses and what we need to develop. The best way to do so is with another quick self-assessment. Please take out your job search journal and answer these five questions:

1. **What are the things you struggle with?**
2. **What does not come naturally to you?**
3. **What tasks drain energy from you?**
4. **What do people say you need to improve on?**
5. **What tasks do you put off or delegate to others?**

Knowing your weaknesses will help determine what may be difficult for you and what you shouldn't do for your career. Maybe you're not organized. Maybe you hate to sit behind a desk and prefer to work outdoors. Perhaps you are shy and have trouble with interpersonal communication; in this case, a customer-facing role would not be the best. However, a desk job like a computer programmer, graphic designer, or financial analyst might actually be more suitable. Of course, that would also depend on your strengths.

Keep in mind that you may be asked the dreaded interview question: "What is your greatest weakness?" You need to be prepared to answer that question, and understanding your weaknesses is the first part of the process.

Since I shared my strength with you, it's only fair that I also share my weakness. Not that I think I have any because none of us ever think we do, LOL. The truth is we all have weaknesses and developmental areas. The only way to truly know what they are is to have an honest conversation with yourself and really think about what they are.

In interviews, people often try to think of how they can spin a positive and make it sound like a negative. We're not doing that here, and I don't recommend you do that in the interview. Be honest with yourself, but be careful not to sabotage yourself in the process.

My weakness, which may seem obvious since you know my strength, is that I tend to be long-winded and indirect. Obviously, for somebody with the gift of gab, it only seems natural that I talk too much. However, the greater problem for me is my lack of brevity. Being direct is important in life, and it's important in business. Brevity is NOT my superpower, something I definitely need to be aware of. I consistently work at this and am fully aware that it's one of my weaknesses.

Important Note: If you have an honest conversation with yourself and still don't feel like you did a good job listing your strengths and weaknesses, find five people you know (and trust) and ask them if they would be willing to give you their honest opinion. Send them an email with the questions I have included in this book and ask them if they can give you their thoughts.

5. Unique Value Proposition (UVP)

Lastly, you need to know your "unique value proposition," or UVP (which is actually a marketing term). Your UVP is what makes you valuable; it's the unique skills and experience that set you apart and differentiate you. Companies will hire you for the value you bring and how valuable you will be to their organization. Put simply, your UVP is like your elevator pitch but to a specific employer. It is a brief overview of your professional background, expertise, accomplishments, and information relevant to your skills and career goals.

Write out your unique value proposition in your job search journal. Before you do, I would like to share my own unique value proposition as an example:

"Accomplished executive search expert with over 25 years of experience as a top talent advisor to the pharmaceutical and biotech industries. Certified speaker, trainer, and coach, as well as podcast host for a globally ranked show dedicated to field medical affairs professionals and pharmaceutical industry leaders. Extensive network of clients, colleagues, professionals, and followers from over 80 countries."

Now it's your turn. Take a moment to write out your UVP. You will need to know it since we will be using it in a later chapter. Don't overthink it or try to make it perfect. It will certainly evolve and go through several iterations, so do your best with your first draft.

So... What Is Your Dream Job?

This is a critical question for your job search. The self-assessment exercises you completed in this chapter should have provided you with the clarity to determine your dream job. It is important to identify your dream job by title. You need to know the exact target because your search will be centered around this specific title. You also need to determine if there are alternate titles associated with the role. Is your dream job called different things? That's going to be very important to know in this process.

My recommendation is to make a list of your dream job titles along with all alternate titles. For example, a medical science liaison can also be called a field medical director, regional scientific manager, senior medical ambassador, and several other things. It all depends on the company. Another example is social media manager, which might also be called brand manager, digital marketing manager, marketing specialist, marketing coordinator, and marketing manager. Many titles will have various names, and I urge you to be aware of this so you can be thorough in your search efforts.

It is important to write this title down, as well as alternate titles, because we are going to use them in another chapter. Also, your dream job is your goal. When you write it out, you make the goal real. It is also important to make it visible to you every day. Revisit the goal and imagine yourself performing in the role. According to Dr. Gail Matthews, a psychology professor at Dominican University in California, you are 42% more likely to achieve your goals just by writing them down.

You just completed a VERY important step in the job search process. Now that you have clarity and know what your dream job is, we can move forward to the next step in the process. I am really excited for you. Let's go!

Chapter 2 Summary

Five-Step Process to Determine Your Dream Job:

- **Vision**
- **Personal Core Values**
- **Strengths and Transferable Skills**
- **Weaknesses and Developmental Area**
- **Unique Value Proposition**

CHAPTER 3

Know the Target

Career Identity

I asked you to evaluate and understand your vision, core values, strengths/transferable skills, weaknesses, and unique value proposition because these five areas are what you will build your career identity around. Career identity, often called "professional identity," is how an individual perceives his/her skills, competencies, values, and motivations with a defined career path or role.

The exercises in Chapter 2 provide the framework to be fully confident in what you want to do next in your career. Such confidence is necessary for you to pursue the goal wholeheartedly.

Another way to describe career identity is to simply ask one question: *What career are you in?*

Answers might be, "I am a college professor," "I am a medical sales representative," or "I am a physical therapist." If I were to ask you the very same question right now, ideally, you would say, "I am a [insert dream job title]." At the very least, you might say, "I am aspiring to be a [dream job title]."

There is a great story of a little boy who went out into his yard with a ball and bat. He said, "I am the best hitter in all the world," threw the ball up in the air, swung the bat as hard as he could, and missed. He took another try, saying, "I am the best hitter in all the world," but again, he swung and missed. Not to be denied, he tried a third time. "I am the best hitter in all the world," he said and swung as hard as he possibly could. He missed so completely this time that he went sprawling in the dirt. Undaunted, he stood up, brushed himself off, and said, "I am the best PITCHER in ALL the world!"

Know the JOB

In today's job market, most employers want subject matter experts rather than utility players. This is a VERY important concept to understand since it will help you tailor your approach. To establish your career identity, you must know ALL there is to know about your dream job. You need to BE an expert even before you ARE an expert. And if you already have experience in your dream job and may be an expert, please stick with me in this chapter. I am going to offer some important information and insights that will help you grow in ways you might not have considered.

Let me start by sharing some inside information I received from a great client. I recently had a conversation with this client, who is a hiring manager for a pharmaceutical company. I asked him, "Paul, what's one of the biggest problems you see in interviews nowadays?"

Paul replied, "One of the biggest problems I see is candidates very often miss the most important details." He went on to say that he asks two questions in every interview: "Why do you want to work for our company?" and "Why do you think you're a good fit for this position?"

Let's talk about the second question: "Why are you a good fit for this position?" Paul shared that he gets very frustrated by applicants' lack of knowledge and understanding of the position they are applying for. This even goes for people with a lot of experience in the role. He wants to see that an applicant has read the job description, knows the responsibilities expected of them, and understands the requirements for the position.

We will discuss this in more detail in the chapter on interviewing, but the important point is to fully know the details of the position and use them to show that you are a great fit for the opportunity and company.

Researching the role and understanding job descriptions are essential steps in the process. You need to know every single detail about your dream job, not just for individual interviews but before you even get started in your job search.

If you have experience and are already an expert in your field, please stick with me. There is a method to my madness. I am going to ask you to complete an important exercise that we will use again later. You *must* complete this step in the process. You will fully understand why in the coming chapters.

Job Description Exercise

The Job Description Exercise includes five steps:

1. **Search career sites on the internet** (Indeed, SimplyHired, LinkedIn, etc.) for your dream job title and print out five job descriptions.

2. **Study each job description and highlight five to seven main *responsibilities* for this position.** Yes, even if you have experience and are an expert in the role, please complete this step.

3. **Study each job description and highlight the five main *requirements* for this position.**

4. **Highlight the keywords, language, and phrases that are repeated in all five job descriptions.**

5. **Make ONE final list of the top five responsibilities, the top five requirements needed for the role, and the top 10 keywords, language, and phrases.** Save this information in your job search journal and save the highlighted job descriptions that you printed out. We will be using this information very soon in our chapter on resumes.

How Qualified Are You?

Now that you have completed the job description exercise, it is important to ask yourself, *How qualified am I for my dream job?* When looking at the main responsibilities and requirements for the role, how many boxes can you check off? Even if you have experience, is there an area where you're lacking or need improvement? It is important to ask these questions because there are ways to build up your skills, competencies, and experience to make you a more attractive candidate.

For example, if your dream job requires you to be at an "advanced" level in MS Excel but you are only "intermediate," you might consider taking a course or getting a certification. One of the things I come across often in my line of work in medical affairs and medical science liaison recruitment is the requirement to prepare and conduct presentations to individuals and groups. For those with limited or no presentations on their resume, I recommend they join Toastmasters International, which is a non-profit organization that helps people develop public speaking skills. The idea is to identify your blind spots and skill gaps. There are plenty of resources and programs available to help you check all the boxes needed to be a strong candidate for your dream job.

Starter Roles (Stepping Stone Positions)

If you feel you have too many skill gaps and you may not be 100% ready for your dream job, it may make sense to find a starter position that will act as a stepping stone. Create a list of potential starter positions that will provide you with the skills and experience to help you develop the competencies needed to compete for your dream job. I know this is a bit anticlimactic and may seem like a waste of time. However, spending a year or two in a starter role is often a great way to establish a foundation for your career identity.

When I graduated college, I wanted to land a role as a pharmaceutical sales rep. Problem was that most positions required prior "business to business" (B2B) sales experience. Not only did I not have B2B sales experience, I had NO experience. I did my research, spoke to friends, and learned the best starter position would be a B2B sales role in healthcare or life sciences. I wound up winning a position as a new business sales rep for US Healthcare (now Aetna). After two full years of selling HMO plans door to door, I started applying for pharmaceutical sales positions. In a short time, I wound up with several offers and accepted a position with Ross Laboratories (now Abbott Labs), where I spent an incredible ten years.

Know the Market

The next step in the pursuit of your career identity is to understand the marketplace and everything there is to know about your dream job industry. You need to learn how to fish in the right pond to catch the right fish, so what I'm going to ask you to do next is research the industry. You need to become an expert on the "market" for your dream job. Even if you have experience, you will benefit from taking a deeper dive.

The next exercise, simply called the "Know the Market Exercise," has four simple steps.

Know the Market Exercise

1. **Search the internet** (NOT career sites) using Google or any other search engine by entering your "dream job title" (in quotes) into the

search bar. You may also want to search using the alternate titles as well. Grab the list we made earlier and put it to use in this exercise if it will be helpful. The goal is to get a sense of the players in the space. Research the results and make a note of the associations, societies, resources, blogs, recruiters, podcasts, coaching programs, certifications, training, etc. You also may want to search for internships or fellowship programs if that is of interest to you at this stage in your career.

2. **Search LinkedIn by dream job title** to see if you can find groups, influencers, companies to follow, and content sources supporting your dream job community. Your dream job may likely have a LinkedIn community already. Become a part of it, and if you already are, double down. We will talk more about engagement with the dream job community in a later chapter.

3. **Search social media channels,** such as Instagram, YouTube, Facebook, X, TikTok, etc., to see if there are dream job communities, groups, influencers, and content sources you can follow.

4. **Make a list of ALL the resources** you just collected so you can start following, joining, engaging, commenting, and fishing in the right pond.

As with Chapter 2, the results of these exercises will be instrumental in your job search. More importantly, they are an investment in your future and will help you create and build your career identity.

I want to take a quick moment to thank you for following along and completing the necessary steps in this process. I would also like to congratulate you on the information you just collected. You will see how it all comes together and builds upon itself later in this book.

Free Download: A Career Planning & Identity Checklist.

Scan the QR code:

Chapter 3 Summary

Know the Target

- **Career Identity**
- **Know the Job**
- **Job Description Exercise**
- **How Qualified Are You?**
- **Starter Roles (Stepping Stone Positions)**
- **Know the Market (Know the Market Exercise)**

CHAPTER 4

Take Aim at the Target

It's time to get your tools ready. Abe Lincoln once said that if he had eight hours to chop down a tree, he would spend six hours sharpening his ax. Well, this is the point where we need to sharpen our ax and all the other tools that are going to help us win our dream job.

Let's start with your resume. Your resume is the cornerstone of your search and the foundation of your career. It is not a once-in-a-while thing. Your resume is a constant work in progress that comes with you every step of your career. Your resume is your ticket to the interview. If it's not written correctly, you will not get a chance to compete.

You need to look at your resume as an investment. It needs to look good, sound good, and be effective. The style and formatting can make or break the first impression. According to the online recruitment platform Qureos, 73% of hiring managers say they are more likely to interview a candidate with a visually appealing resume. You also need to tell a story. Every word counts, so carefully consider the way it looks and sounds.

However, the best-looking resumes can still fail. It is critical to make sure your resume is optimized to get through applicant tracking system filters and artificial intelligence screenings. The key to success with your resume is that it needs to be targeted specifically to your dream job. Not only is it important to get through ATS filters, but 83% of recruiters say they're more likely to hire a candidate who has tailored their resume to the specific job they're applying for.

According to a study of 133,000 resumes done by the resume-building website Zety, only 10% of job applications actually result in interview invites. So, your resume is actually a moving target. It's not a one-size-fits-all document. It needs to be tailored specifically to each and every job you pursue. To be clear, and to use a technical term, you need to create a *high-converting resume*. This means a resume that will make it through applicant tracking system filters and convert to interviews.

I would like to share the story of Melissa, one of the members of our coaching program. I learned this week that Melissa applied to positions for eight months without landing one interview. She was concerned her resume was not written or optimized properly. Clearly, it was not converting. One of the first steps in our program is a complete resume revision and rewrite using the proper formatting and resume-tailoring techniques I will outline in this book. Melissa explained that after completing our course, she started to get responses and now has a final interview for her dream job (six weeks from the time she first joined us).

Understanding Applicant Tracking System Filters

Have you ever applied to a bunch of jobs and never heard back? Do you feel like your resume just got stuck in a big black hole of resumes? Before writing or revamping your resume, you need to understand applicant tracking systems. An applicant tracking system (ATS) is a database that helps companies organize candidates for hiring and recruitment purposes. ATSs are equipped with screening and filtering capabilities through algorithms, which is a form of artificial intelligence, or AI. ATSs will filter or screen out resumes based on keywords or lack thereof.

Importance of Keywords

Resume keywords are descriptive words or phrases that relate to job function. They are the abilities, skills, expertise, and values that the recruiter is looking for in a candidate. Keywords are the foundation of a search string for recruiters and hiring managers.

One of the most important keywords or phrases is the dream job title itself. Whether you currently perform in that function or have yet to gain experience in your dream job, you still need to be sure the keyword "dream job title" exists somewhere on your resume. For example, use the exact job title listed on the job description. Hiring teams conduct searches using titles. Applicant tracking systems may also include the dream job title as a keyword in their algorithm, which makes it super important for it to be on your resume in order to convert. I will show you a great place to add your dream job title in the next section.

Important Note: The reason I asked you to complete the job description exercise in Chapter 2 is that we will be using the highlighted keywords, language, and phrases to make your resume relevant to your dream job. This is called "skill matching."

How to Get Your Resume Through Applicant Tracking System Filters

Skill matching is the activity of "matching" your skills and experience to a specific job description using keywords, phrases, and language. Be careful not to document something on your resume that you cannot support. You must be able to prove any and all information on your resume. Do not overuse keywords. Applicant tracking systems will pick up the overuse of keywords, which is a violation.

Be careful when using artificial intelligence tools to do skill matching. There are ways of using ChatGPT to do the skill-matching exercise for you, and there are tools, such as SkillSyncer and Jobscan, that do it as well. I'm not saying that these tools are not effective, but I advise extreme caution if you decide to use an AI tool because YOU need to be the one to prove every single claim you make. In my experience, things get overstated and are inaccurate after using AI. Just remind yourself when skill matching that if you didn't do it, you can't document it.

Don't try to trick the applicant tracking system by hiding keywords. This is not a new idea, and it will not help you. Hiding keywords means adding phrases, language, and even full job descriptions into the white space of your resume and then changing the font color to white. This will make those keywords invisible but still present. This is an old trick that people used many years ago to get more keywords onto their resume, but applicant tracking systems now convert all text to black and pick up on all documented text. Recruiters are aware of this as well, so whenever we see areas of white space, we will convert all text to black and catch you in the act. At that point, it's game over.

There are a few other important rules to keep in mind. Applicant tracking systems do not pick up tables, text boxes, vertical text, logos, images, graphics, columns, headers, footers, uncommon fonts, or uncommon sections. To be clear, any content like that is not going to be credited by the applicant tracking system filter. This is important to keep in mind when writing and revising your resume. It is common for people to add important information into headers and footers or overuse text boxes. The ATS will not credit anything in these areas. Fancy and more stylistic resume templates will have many of these features, so be mindful of where critical information resides in the document.

The best file types to save your resume as would be DOCX and PDF format. Some experts suggest always sending your resume as a PDF since the formatting will not change in transit, which can sometimes happen with other file formats. I would say stick to PDF, but if an applicant tracking system suggests a different file type, use the one specified.

When you save your resume, just use your first and last name, followed by "resume." Do not put a date or any other descriptions. If you do, it may show how long you've been on the job market, which is never beneficial, especially if it resurfaces at a later time in the search process.

The Most Important Section of Your Resume

The top half of the first page is the most important section of your resume. This is what is called "above the fold" on your computer, meaning you don't need to scroll down to see any further information. According to a Forbes.com article, Recruiters can spend as little as six to eight seconds reviewing a resume. That means many are just scanning them, so the top portion must be compelling to grab the reader's attention.

In the top half of the first page of your resume, there will be three sections: Contact information, Professional Summary, and Core Competencies.

Contact Information

As I mentioned earlier, the ATS will not pick up information in the margins, which includes the header and footer. My advice is to shrink the margin on the top and add your contact information on the actual document, not in the header. The contact information is very simple: first name, last name, and credentials. If you have a PhD, PharmD, MBA, or whatever certifications, make sure to include those. You're also going to add your city and state (not your physical street address), your email address, one phone number (mobile is preferred), and a link to your LinkedIn profile (this is called your Public Profile URL).

Please have a professional email for your resume. Do not have an email such as "beerbellybob@hotmail.com." According to a study by CareerBuilder, 76% of resumes are ignored if candidates have an unprofessional email address. Some experts suggest switching from Hotmail, AOL, and even Yahoo email addresses since they are very outdated service providers. An "out of touch" or less sophisticated job applicant is not as desirable, so you may want to opt for a Gmail address to provide better optics.

Professional Summary

Directly under your contact information is going to be a Professional Summary, not an objective. In my opinion, objectives are a bit passé and not the best use of that space. A 2023 survey by CareerBuilder found that only 37% of recruiters say that they look for a resume objective. However, you can add an objective in the last sentence of your professional summary. This is also the perfect place to add a keyword as your dream job title. I have included an example below.

Why is the Professional Summary so important? Again, much of the reader's time is going to be spent on the top half of the first page. Your professional summary is going to make the first impression. It may also be the last impression. The reader may actually spend more time looking at the professional summary than anything else. Also, according to a 2022 survey by LinkedIn, 72% of hiring managers say that they are more likely to hire a candidate who has a well-written *summary* of their skills and experience. Ideally, you want this section to be a paragraph of three to six sentences, depending on your experience.

Now, here is where we start tying some things together. I want you to state your UVP, unique value proposition, in your professional summary. You should have this ready to go from our earlier exercise. If you remember the example I gave of my UVP, here's what it might look like translated into a professional summary:

> *"Accomplished executive search expert with over 25 years of experience as a top talent advisor to the pharmaceutical and biotech industries. Certified speaker, trainer, and coach, as well as podcast host for a globally ranked show dedicated to field medical affairs professionals and pharmaceutical industry leaders. Extensive network of clients, colleagues, professionals, and followers from over 80 countries. Seeking a position as a (dream job title) with a growing organization."*

That's a good example of a professional summary. You will notice that the last sentence acts as an objective. This is optional, but it's a great place to include your dream job title if you do not have it elsewhere in the resume. I must again stress the importance of the Professional Summary. It will be the first impression you make on a recruiter or hiring manager and must be impactful.

Core Competencies

The very next section, under the Professional Summary, is Core Competencies. These include your transferable skills, and the need to include them is one of the reasons why I asked you to complete the exercise in Chapter 2.

This section has a very important purpose. It is not just to showcase your skills but is also a great place to include keywords specific to your dream job. So, we will now use the list of transferable skills in addition to the highlighted keywords, language, and phrases from the Job Description exercise. Any keywords you have yet to include on your resume should go into your Core Competencies.

It is sufficient to put eight to 12 skills in that section. This is important because you will get keyword recognition for those skills, which can help your resume with ATS conversions. Keep in mind that you do not want to overuse keywords, so when your resume is complete, double-check that you used all the right words and phrases without overusing them. The skills should be written in rows and columns rather than as a list. If you have ten words, use five rows and two columns. If you have nine, use three rows and three columns. This is both to save space and to look more appealing.

Example:

TOM CARAVELA

Montville, New Jersey 02123 | Email: tcaravela44@gmail.com | Phone: (444) 333-8989

PROFESSIONAL SUMMARY

Accomplished executive search expert with over 25 years of experience as a top talent advisor to the pharmaceutical and biotech industries. Certified speaker, trainer, and coach, as well as podcast host for a globally ranked show dedicated to field medical affairs professionals and pharmaceutical industry leaders. Extensive network of clients, colleagues, professionals, and followers from over 80 countries. Seeking a position as a (dream job title) with a growing organization.

CORE COMPETENCIES

- Account Acquisition/Management
- Written and Oral Communication
- Leadership and Strategic Planning
- Collaborative Learning

- Relationship Development
- Contract Negotiations
- Team Building
- Prospecting/Outreach

- Idea Development
- Creating/Formatting Documents
- Analytical and Strategic Thinking
- Organizational Skills

Professional Experience

After the Core Competencies section, we are going to put Professional Experience. This is also known as the body of your resume. The key to this section is not just documenting your responsibilities; it is showcasing your success and the impact you have made in an organization. According to LinkedIn, 75% of hiring managers want to see specific accomplishments and results in the work experience section.

There is a very specific format that I would like you to follow when you are documenting your Professional Experience. Most people use bullets, but you can also list the information in sentences. Either way, here is the format you will want to follow:

Action verb + specific task/responsibility + quantifiable result (outcome/accomplishments)

What are action verbs? Action verbs are words like spearheaded, orchestrated, chaired, organized, produced, etc. It is important to start your bullets or sentences with a strong action verb. According to Jennifer Herrity, writing for Indeed.com, "Action verbs are words that express an action. In a resume, action verbs are used to highlight your skills, experience and accomplishments. They are specific, clarify your contributions and bring a confident tone to your resume. Using action verbs that are unique and powerful can increase your chances of capturing the attention of an employer and moving to the next step in the hiring process." (Source: Indeed.com)

Free Download: List of Action Verbs for Resume Writing.

Scan the QR code:

Here's an example of a well-written bullet:

- *Developed (action verb) a collaboration with a key vendor (specific task) that resulted in a successful partnership that saved the company X amount of dollars (quantifiable result).*

To determine your quantifiable results, ask these questions:

- How have I saved my company money?
- How have I generated revenue for my company?
- How have I improved the process, system, operations, etc.?
- How have I found a solution to a problem?
- What accomplishments am I most proud of?

People seem to have a very difficult time determining quantifiable results, but what you really need to do is take a look at prior resumes, prior projects, and where you were able to make an impact in the organization. The questions above should act as a good guide.

If you are an entry-level job seeker with limited experience, this section can prove to be more challenging. However, you can apply the same guidelines for any internships, starter positions, fellowships, or even volunteer work. Potential employers are impressed by results, value, impact, and how your efforts contributed to the success of the organization.

Length of Your Resume

One of the most common questions when it comes to resumes is: "How long should my resume be? Should it only be one page? Should it only be two pages?" There are several considerations to determine what might be best for you. First, the length of your resume should have a direct correlation to the number of years of experience you have. If you have 30 years of experience, you do not want to shortchange yourself with a one-page resume. If you have no experience and this is your first job, you should not have a six-page resume, so keep it to one. It's pretty simple.

You are going to hear resume writing experts and career coaches tell you that it's career suicide to have a resume longer than one or two pages. I do not agree with this. I think that you want to have a resume that's going to do the best job of highlighting your skills, experience, and why you are valuable to an organization.

That said, how much you need to include really depends on your experience and your industry. Certain industries and jobs require more sections in a resume. For example, if you work in the pharmaceutical industry as a medical science liaison, you will need to demonstrate your written and verbal communication skills. You may want to add a list of presentations, publications, articles, etc. These extra sections will certainly add to the length but are necessary.

Conversely, financial firms and some larger companies ONLY want to see a one-page resume. The reason is simple: employers must screen hundreds of resumes at times, so having a short, concise resume allows for better efficiency. According to Indeed, 63% of hiring managers say they prefer resumes that are one page long. My advice is to know the expectations of your job and industry while taking into consideration your tenure; I am sure you will make the right call.

Resume "Dos" and "Don'ts"

- Do pick a professional template that highlights your expertise properly.
- Do highlight tenure and career stability.
- Do proofread, spellcheck, and ask others to help you look it over.

- Do have multiple versions if you have several unique value propositions.
- Do be 100% truthful and able to support any and all claims.
- Do update your resume at least twice each year. Quarterly is recommended.
- Do not use "I," "me," or "my" in your resume.

To be more specific, you want to write your resume in the first person but not use "I," "me," or "my." You're not writing it as if you're someone else; you're writing it in the first person, but you're not using "I" or "me." And you need to be consistent with that language throughout the entire document. If you remember my unique value proposition, which is also my professional summary, you will see I do not refer to myself as "I" or "me."

Top Resume Mistakes to Avoid

According to CareerBuilder, 77% of recruiters see typos or poor grammar as dealbreakers, and 35% feel the same about unprofessional email addresses. A large global study by McKinsey found that 60% of recruiters say that the biggest mistake job seekers make on their resumes is using too many buzzwords. 68% of hiring managers say they would reject a candidate because of a poorly formatted resume (Source: Qureos) And according to job site The Ladders, a photograph might distract recruiters from the resume's actual contents, and around 88% of resumes are rejected for including one.

Multiple Versions

It is acceptable to have multiple versions of your resume as long as you can support any and all claims you are making. The reason to have more than one version is when you have different specialties or want to highlight certain skills or experience to better fit the job description. Maybe you are an accountant who specializes in tax planning, so you have a very detailed "tax" resume in addition to a more general resume.

As we discussed, I advise tailoring your resume to each job description, which may mean several versions that are all similar but highlight different areas of specialty depending on the job. Be very careful to remember which version you send to which company. And again, be 100% sure you can support ALL claims you are making.

Cover Letters (When to Use Them and How)

Cover letters are designed to briefly state why you are a good fit for a specific position and provide pertinent details on your candidacy for the role and your interest level. The letter is an introduction that supports the resume; it does not replace it. Be careful not to just repeat what is said on your resume. You will only want to highlight how you are a fit for the role.

You do NOT want to add your cover letter to the beginning of your resume, which people sometimes do. The cover letter is a separate document. The best way to use your cover letter is to copy and paste it into the body of an email when you are sending your resume to someone. Otherwise, simply add it as an attachment.

If you are applying online to a position, and it gives you the option to add a cover letter, I recommend doing so. You want to use the opportunity to offer extra information that can help tell your story and make you a more attractive candidate vs. the competition. Some might say cover letters are a waste of time and that no one reads them anymore. Perhaps, but in the event a key piece of information in the cover letter catches the eye of the right person, it could prove to be effective.

I heard a story from someone who recently landed her dream job after many months of searching. Her name is Cindy and she explained that she had applied to 70 positions before landing her first interview. Luckily for Cindy, she was offered and accepted the position after completing several interviews. The hiring manager told her that one of the key factors was her cover letter. Cindy said she had added a personal touch by mentioning she and her husband are avid animal lovers and live in a rural area where they care for their five rescue dogs. It was a brief and simple added personal touch that she was compelled to include. The hiring manager told her that even though she was less qualified than some of the other applicants, she felt a bit of a connection and was compelled to have a conversation with her. Cindy did the rest to win the job!

Portfolios, Brag Books, and Journals

Having a portfolio, "brag book," or journal as a supplement to your resume can be extremely helpful, depending on the industry. This could be a bound book of select accomplishments you want to highlight. It might be your portfolio if you're a graphic designer. It might be a list of awards if you're a salesperson. Or it could be just a journal of some of the highlights, projects, and accomplishments you have achieved throughout your career. You can even be very junior and have a brief career journal if, perhaps, you worked an internship or did a fellowship where you were involved in some exciting projects.

Providing such an addendum of accomplishments, achievements, and experience is not mandatory. However, it could separate you from other job seekers, so be aware that while it is not required, it is a helpful way to prove how good you actually are. This supplement can be something you leave behind if you are able to make multiple copies. In some cases, a portfolio of work is used as an example only and not something that can be copied or left behind.

Artificial Intelligence

Artificial intelligence can be a very helpful tool for your job search. I am sure it will continue to evolve considerably in years to come, so whatever I say may be outdated by the time you read this. However, I want to be sure to mention that you need to use these tools with caution. Artificial intelligence is useful, but it's not necessarily aware of everything in your brain, nor does it know everything you've accomplished. Only you know that. So, be careful to make sure the information produced by the machine is 100% accurate. YOU need to be the final determiner of what you document and how it is communicated to a potential employer.

> **Disclaimer:** Artificial intelligence was NOT used to write this book. What you are reading came from my crazy brain and includes my experience, knowledge, and collective learnings from a long career in the job search and placement business. ☺

Chapter 4 Summary

Take Aim at the Target

- Your Resume: The Cornerstone of Your Search and the Foundation of Your Career
- Understanding Applicant Tracking System Filters
- Importance of Keywords
- How to Get Your Resume Through Applicant Tracking System Filters
- Skill Matching
- The Most Important Section of Your Resume

- Contact Information, Professional Summary, Professional Experience
- Bullet or "Body of Resume" Formula: Action Verb + Specific Task/Responsibility + Quantifiable Result
- Length of Your Resume
- Resume Dos and Don'ts
- Top Resume Mistakes to Avoid
- Multiple Versions
- Cover Letters
- Portfolios, Brag Books, and Journals
- Artificial Intelligence Tools

CHAPTER 5

LinkedIn: The Most Important Tool in the Shed

Now that your resume is complete, all bright and shiny and ready to go, it is time to tackle LinkedIn. Why is LinkedIn so important? At the time of this writing, LinkedIn is the single greatest resource available to professionals, entrepreneurs, students, and anyone looking to establish a career. It is a public display of your resume, an advertisement of your professional experience, and a huge part of your digital brand. It is a way to see and be seen by other professionals. LinkedIn is also a job board that can average 20 million job postings at any given time. LinkedIn is the perfect networking resource.

As of June 2023, LinkedIn had more than 930 million members across 200-plus countries and territories worldwide (according to LinkedIn 2023 statistics). Anyone and everyone in the professional world is on LinkedIn, and you should be, too. It is arguably the single greatest tool to establish your digital brand and professional image.

Let me explain what happens when a recruiter (like me), hiring manager, or talent acquisition professional receives your resume. The very next thing we do is go to your LinkedIn profile to see what your profile picture looks like, what your personal/professional brand is, and if your profile accurately matches your resume.

Do titles, companies, and dates match up? What content are you posting, and how does it display your brand? What sort of engagement do you have, and how many followers or connections? We will look at everything on your profile that will help us better understand if you are a job seeker we want to pursue. However, keep in mind that it is likely that the very first time a recruitment professional comes across your LinkedIn profile, it's because we are actually searching for a candidate just like you, or you just happen to wind up in our feed.

So, your profile is the very first impression that we get, not your resume. This is why I cannot stress enough the importance of your LinkedIn profile and your engagement and continued participation on the platform.

Where to Start… Paid vs. Free

The very first thing I advise you to do is purchase a premium LinkedIn package. The LinkedIn basic plan is free, so you don't have to spend money to be on the platform. That means there is no reason not to participate, even if money is an issue. That said, I highly recommend upgrading to a premium plan.

Currently, LinkedIn offers a Premium Career Plan, which is a common choice for many job seekers like you. They also offer a LinkedIn Premium Business Plan, which may be a little pricey for some users, but it does offer more features. According to LinkedIn statistics, job seekers with a LinkedIn Premium Career account get hired two times faster than those with a free account.

Please Note: I am not affiliated with LinkedIn or benefit from this advice in any monetary fashion. The opinions shared in this book are strictly based on my professional experience and best practices to aid in your success.

The FREE LinkedIn basic plan is limiting because:

1. The plan does not allow you to in-mail (direct message) people you are not connected to. You must have a first-degree connection with a person to send them a direct message.

2. You can't always see who visits your profile. That feature only comes with a paid membership. Sometimes, it's helpful to see who's actually checking you out on LinkedIn, especially when you're in the middle of a job search.

3. Without a premium plan, your searches are limited.

One reason I suggest an upgrade to a LinkedIn premium plan is that you can get in-mails each month and communicate with people directly, and the better functionality of such plans will help you in your search efforts. Currently, the LinkedIn Premium Career Plan will actually give you five in-mails per month. The LinkedIn Premium Business Plan will give you 15 per month.

Setting Up and Optimizing Your LinkedIn Profile

Many of you are already on LinkedIn. Probably some of you are also very active on LinkedIn. However, whether you have a profile set up or not, I advise you to read this entire chapter because I'm going to give you some current best practices and tips that may help your existing profile or be a great asset if you're creating one from scratch. It's important to know that LinkedIn often makes changes to its platform. By the time you read this, there could be different titles, rules, parameters, pricing, etc. What I am sharing with you is based on my experience and knowledge at present.

LinkedIn vs. Resume

The very first thing to know is your LinkedIn profile is NOT your resume. It is a much more robust asset that allows you to showcase more content than your resume. That said, you will want to be consistent in your messaging and language with both assets. In the same way that you targeted your dream job on your resume, you will want to do the same thing on your LinkedIn profile.

The same principles that you used to create your highly converting resume, you also need to use for LinkedIn. Why? LinkedIn is a searchable platform. Recruitment professionals are on LinkedIn all day, every day, doing searches and trying to find people to fill their open positions, so your LinkedIn profile's keywords, phrases, and language must be aligned with your dream job so you can be found when recruitment professionals are searching for someone like you.

It's very important to make sure your LinkedIn profile is complete. LinkedIn will actually tell you what percentage of your profile has been completed. For example, it might say that it's 70% complete, 80% complete, etc. I recommend you follow the LinkedIn guide and instructions so you can fully complete your profile.

Header (Including the Banner and Photo)

Your banner should relate to what you are driving towards and clearly explain who you are or what people can expect from you. The banner is an image that sits behind your photo. The image can be related to your dream job and what you want people to think about you. It can be a great branding tool. If you're a scientist, you can put something that says science. If you're a graphic artist, you could have something very creative that exemplifies your style.

Your LinkedIn photo is a very important piece of the equation. Why? Because recruitment professionals will go to LinkedIn to see what you look like. I know that sounds crazy, but it's true. We want to see if your photo is aligned with your digital brand and your dream job. Your photo should be professional, edited, and close up.

LinkedIn is not Facebook. It should not be a personal photo of you and your significant other or you holding up a pint of beer toasting your friends. It should be a professional headshot. However, it's better to have an imperfect photo than none at all. Not having a LinkedIn photo creates a bad impression because it leaves the visitor wondering, "Why does this person not want to be seen?" or "Is this person too lazy to get around to adding a photo?"

I recommend creating a current professional headshot, even if it is from a cell phone. Avoid over editing or using an old photo since it may be jarring for people when you meet them in a live, professional setting. I do not recommend using a photo created by artificial intelligence, even if it is impossible to tell it is not a real photo. Sites like LinkedIn can now identify fake or artificial profiles and photos.

You can portray your dream job in your photo. For example, if you're a scientist and looking for a job in a lab, it might not be a bad idea to have a photo of you in a lab coat. But if you're a scientist working in the lab and you're looking to transition to a corporate role, you should ditch the lab coat for something more professional. I offer the same advice to college students. If you want to become a medical sales rep, take down the photo of you in your cap and gown, holding up your diploma. Why? Because you look like a student and not a medical sales rep. Replace the grad pic with you in a business suit so you look the part. Convince others you are ready for your dream job, and better yet, convince yourself.

Title/Headline

You have an opportunity to brand yourself in the title/headline section by using the right keywords and phrases that are going to best describe you. LinkedIn currently gives you a maximum of 120 characters in this section, and it is important to use them to highlight who you are and what makes you special. It's not a bad idea to visit the profiles of people who are doing the same job that you want to do and get some examples of how they describe themselves (without plagiarizing).

This is a highly visible section, so you should use descriptive words and phrases that will make a great first impression. This section is not just a place to add a title. It's a place to showcase your career identity, your unique value proposition, and what makes you most attractive as a professional. What do you do? Who do you serve? What makes you special? How are you valuable?

Example: (my LinkedIn Header):

Top Talent Advisor & Job Search Expert. Keynote Speaker, Trainer, Coach. Podcast Host & Best Selling Author 🙂

My advice would be to check profiles of others in your dream job space to get ideas of what you might want to say in your own header.

Public Profile URL (Personal Link)

LinkedIn allows you to create a custom Public Profile URL, which is a personal link to your profile. It's actually very simple to do. First, click the "Me" icon at the top of your LinkedIn homepage. Then click "View Profile." Once you are on your profile page, click the "Edit" icon next to "Public Profile & URL" on the right pane.

When creating the link, people usually include their name, but you can also customize it to include what you want to portray. For example, my LinkedIn profile URL is https://www.linkedin.com/in/tomcaravela-executiverecruiter/. You can make it say whatever you want, and once you have this personal link, you can use it on your resume or in an email if you want to direct someone to your LinkedIn profile.

Contact Info

One of the most often missed but very important parts of your profile is contact information. As a recruiter, I cannot tell you how many times I've been on someone's LinkedIn profile and not been able to find an email address or a phone number anywhere. Don't let this be you.

Including the information is very simple to do. Just make sure you state how best to contact you. The information should be the same as on your resume. Some people leave this information out on purpose because they do not want to open themselves up to solicitation. I can understand that. But if you are a job seeker in the middle of an active search, be sure to give people a way to contact you. Otherwise, you could potentially miss out on opportunities.

About Section

The LinkedIn "About" section, previously the "Summary" section, is a perfect place to add more detailed content than you have on your resume. This section currently allows for 2,600 characters, which gives you plenty of real estate to tell a compelling story about yourself. Just look at this section as your professional summary on steroids. You may want to incorporate pieces of your cover letter as well. Showcase who you are and what you want people to know about you.

This section is one of the main differentiators from your resume. Share something about your authentic self. Do not be overly personal, as you might risk making it unprofessional, but certainly take more liberties than you would on your resume.

It is important to note that there is a chance the reader only sees this section of your LinkedIn. It might be the only place they look, so make this section count. Again, tell a story and leave the visitor impressed. You can also add contact info in this section, something like, "The best way to reach me is (222) 333-4444 or email ace@dreamjob.com." That way, if they missed your contact info in the other section, it will be clearly stated here as well.

Skills

You're going to use this section to add your Core Competencies and keywords that you already have on your resume. Don't overthink this. As a matter of fact, I would max out this section to the best of your ability. This is another section on LinkedIn that allows you to add much more than you would on your resume. I believe you are able to choose up to 50 skills. LinkedIn breaks the section into four categories:

- **Industry Knowledge**
- **Tools and Technologies**
- **Interpersonal Skills**
- **Other Skills**

Click through each category and select the most relevant skills for your dream job. As a guide, think about the important keywords, language, and phrases associated with your dream job. LinkedIn will provide the options for you to select, so be sure to pick the ones that best portray your career identity and dream job goals.

Experience and Education

LinkedIn gives you a place to add your professional experience. For this section, I recommend you add exactly what you have in the experience section of your resume. Potential employers and recruiters will look to see if the information on your profile matches your resume. Any discrepancies may raise a red flag and create questions. To prevent that from happening, copy and paste right from your resume and into this section. Make sure the dates and timelines match as well.

Go from company to company, experience to experience, in populating this section. In the "Education" section, you will do the same thing: copy and paste from your resume. Once completing these sections, you should have a complete mirror image of your resume for these areas.

Featured

The "Featured" section is located near the top of your profile, and it allows you to feature documents such as resumes, PowerPoints, images, etc. You could also add a recent post or any other content you have created on LinkedIn. Unlike your resume, this is a place to show examples of your work, and it provides the perfect opportunity to highlight your brand.

Use this section to show people your digital presence and how you are aligned with your dream job. I recommend being specific about what you share with people in this section. Make sure the content you choose to "feature" is in line with your dream job and professional brand. This section is very visible, and the thumbnails you use can be eye-catching, so make the most of them.

Building Your Network

Building out your LinkedIn network is crucial. Currently, LinkedIn will allow you to have 30,000 connections. The site limits you to a maximum of 100 invites per week, but you can have an unlimited amount of followers. My advice is to connect with anyone and everyone in your personal and professional worlds. Yes, you want to connect with everyone you know. Building your network is a key strategy for success in your search.

A simple daily practice would be to send a LinkedIn connection request immediately after a business meeting or conversation. Make it a point to visit the person's LinkedIn profile within 24 hours and invite them to connect. It's an important best practice for your career, and it's something that will help build your network over time.

LinkedIn Daily Action Plan for Connections

- Send out 10 to 15 LinkedIn Connection Invites per day with a target of 75 to 100 per week.

I do not recommend putting this off until the weekend. It will be too difficult to bang out a hundred invites on a Saturday and or Sunday. This is a great career habit to adopt and a huge investment for your future. *It also ties into a key strategy that I will share with you in the next chapter.*

There is another reason this LinkedIn Daily Action Plan is so important: it's PROGRESS! This is exactly what progress looks like. How good are you going to feel each day after you complete the exercise of getting your LinkedIn invites out? How good are you going to feel when people start accepting those invites? How good are you going to feel as you watch your network grow and grow and grow?

How to Send LinkedIn Connection Invites

One of the best ways to get more people to accept your invites is to include a personalized note. LinkedIn gives you the option to send the invite with or without a note. Sometimes, you may know the person well or just had a conversation with them, so a note may not be necessary. A best practice, whenever possible, is to include a personalized note, especially if you do not know the person.

It is important to give them a reason to connect with you. Perhaps you have a mutual colleague, connection, or someone who referred you. You may have something in common, such as a school, background, area of study, specialty, etc. My advice is to make your note brief yet personalized. An example might be:

Hi, Joe. I was referred to you by Linda Smith, who mentioned your expertise in [X]. I would like to add you to my professional network and hope to be a resource for you in the future.

The key is to mention something that will not come off as a solicitation or a favor. Make yourself familiar in some way.

Another reason you want to add as many connections as possible is to save in-mails. To clarify, an in-mail is a direct message on the LinkedIn platform. When you are a 1st-degree connection with someone, you are not charged for that direct message. This leaves you with more in-mails for people you are not first-degree connections with. It also means your content will come up on their feed once you are first-degree connections.

There's a much more important reason to add as many people as possible to your network. We'll get to that in the next chapter.

LinkedIn Engagement for Visibility

There's building your network, and then there's "engagement" with your network. Engagement happens after you connect. Let me tell you a story about Gary Johnson. I met Gary very early in his job search. He was a smart guy but had no experience. He was very credentialed and wanted to transition into his dream job in the pharmaceutical industry.

Gary was on my LinkedIn feed every day. Gary liked, commented, and shared many of my posts, including all of my podcast announcements and all of my daily content. I knew Gary without knowing Gary. He became familiar and relevant to me even though I didn't know who he was. I just kept seeing him every day. Quite honestly, he was so supportive and complimentary regarding my content that I almost felt indebted to him.

One day, I got a direct message from Gary telling me how much he appreciated my content and how helpful it was to him. He didn't ask me for anything. There was no call to action. He just wanted to say thank you. That resonated with me. I felt like I wanted to help this guy. A few weeks later, Gary reached out to me again. Meanwhile, every day, he was in my feed, liking, commenting, and sharing. This time, his message had a call to action. He wanted me to take a look at his resume to see what my opinion was. How could I say no? It was the least I could do.

A couple of weeks after I helped Gary with his resume, he sent me another direct message, this time asking me if I would "be able to spare just a few minutes" of my valuable time to do an informational interview. Of course, I was happy to do it. Why? We had developed a professional relationship. I saw his face on my feed every single day. That was the only reason I knew Gary. No one had introduced me to him. He was a stranger before those encounters.

Well, don't you know, Gary eventually landed his dream job. And just last year, he was named Rookie of the Year for 2023 in his dream job. Gary is a superstar. He did everything right.

Engage Like Gary

It is important to visit LinkedIn each day and engage with your connections as well as others in your dream job community. Daily engagement creates visibility. You will want to find the influencers in your dream job space (hiring managers, recruiters, leaders, and potential colleagues) and start engaging.

Here are some of the different ways you can create visibility through engagement:

- **Likes:** Add "likes," or what LinkedIn calls "reactions," to current posts of influencers.

- **Comments:** Add comments and contribute to discussions.

- **Shares:** Click the share button to circulate posts that may benefit your dream job community.

- **Celebrations:** LinkedIn shows promotions and new job announcements. Offer congratulations daily for career announcements.

- **Birthdays:** Some users will add a birthday, so be sure to say, *"Happy Birthday!"* to key contacts.

- **Endorsements:** You can endorse someone for skills (industry knowledge, tools, technologies, interpersonal skills).

- **Recommendations:** These are not the same as endorsements. LinkedIn offers a way to write a letter of recommendation right on the person's profile.

- **Polls:** Some influencers post weekly or monthly polls. Be a regular participant and contributor.
- **LinkedIn Live:** Seek out webinars and live events hosted by influencers in your dream job space. This is not only a way to be visible but also to interact with influencers (since most of these sessions offer a Q&A session at the end).

Gary Johnson was masterful at engagement. He was also consistent and spent time each day on all of the above-mentioned LinkedIn activities. It is not incredibly hard to do. Actually, it's easy. Like anything else, it takes a time commitment and proper planning. This is why I am so insistent on scheduling these actions by chunking time each day.

LinkedIn Daily Action Plan for Engagement

- Go to 10 different influencer profiles or hashtags of people in your dream job community and comment on each. Then, respond to 10 commenters on those accounts.
- Go to 10 of your ideal contacts in your dream job community and comment on their posts.

This engagement will put you front and center in your dream job community, and you will start to get noticed. You will also learn a lot and educate yourself on the latest trends in your dream job space. Being active in the community is a great career habit and investment in your future.

Free Download: LinkedIn Secrets and Content Strategies article.

Scan the QR code:

Chapter 5 Summary

LinkedIn: The Most Important Tool in the Shed

- Where to Start… Paid vs. Free
- Setting Up and Optimizing Your LinkedIn profile
    - LinkedIn vs. Resume
    - Header (Including the Banner and Photo)
    - Title/Headline
    - Public Profile URL (Personal Link)
    - Contact Information
    - About Section
    - Skills, Experience, and Education
    - Featured
    - Building Your network
    - LinkedIn Daily Action Plan for Connections
    - How to Send Out LinkedIn Connection Invites
    - LinkedIn Engagement for Visibility
    - Engage Like Gary
    - LinkedIn Daily Action Plan for Engagement

CHAPTER 6

Job Search Process Roadmap: Navigating Your Path to Success

You have reached the chapter that holds the secret sauce of this entire book. No, it is not a shortcut or a workaround. No, it is not a quick fix or cheat code. This is the strategy that will work if executed properly and with daily consistent action. It is still only one piece of a larger puzzle and does take some time to develop. But here is where we start to get strategic in our search.

Step 1: The Search

You will begin by using career development sites such as Indeed, Simply Hired, Career Builder, Monster, and, of course, LinkedIn, or whatever other internet sites will show you active job postings. Rather than doing individual job searches each day, I recommend you set up "Job Alerts" for the sites that offer it so the research actually comes to you.

Here's how it works:

1. Go to indeed.com (for example).
2. Type "[your dream job title]" (in quotes) in the search box, for example, "medical science liaison," and select a location.

3. Click "Search" for results.

4. Create a "Job Alert" with that search criteria by adding your email address. Setting up this alert means that each day, all new job postings for that criteria will be emailed to you automatically. The nice thing about this is that all of the research comes to you. Now, I still advise researching individual websites and companies so you leave no stone unturned. If you're following a specific company you want to work for, it's a great idea to visit it regularly to see what new positions have been posted. But to save yourself some time, creating job alerts and having some automation in the process cuts down on the amount of time you have to spend doing this. I recommend you follow the same basic instructions for Indeed with Simply Hired and LinkedIn, both of which offer job alerts. You can certainly try to set them up for as many sites as you can.

Step 2: Job Inventory Spreadsheet

Create a Job Inventory Spreadsheet to keep track of the opportunities you wish to pursue. This is a very important way to stay organized and efficient throughout the process. Your spreadsheet should include the job title, company, location or territory, posting date, contact person (if available), and the date you applied for the position.

This is a very crucial step in the process. It is an investment for not only your current job search but your future since, at some point, you may be on the job market again and will need to revisit this document.

Example: (Job Inventory Spreadsheet)

	A	B	C	D	E	F	G	H
1	Date Posted	Job Title	Company	Location	Contact Person	Date Applied	Source	Notes/Actions
2	July 1, 2023	Medical Science Liaison	XYZ Company	Field Based-NJ, NY	Rachel Green	July 4th, 2023	Indeed	No connections on LI
3	July 1, 2023	Clinical Application Specialist	ABC Company	Field Based-CA, AZ	Ross Geller	July 5th, 2023	LI	Emailed Phoebe Snow-works in Med Info department
4								
5								

Important Note: To stay organized, use your Job Inventory Spreadsheet from the very beginning of your search so you can keep track of where and when you apply. Do not expect to rely on your own memory; it will not work. When you obtain a contact person's name, document it on the spreadsheet. When you make progress, document it on the spreadsheet. When you follow up with someone, document it on the spreadsheet.

Details are key and need to be captured along the way. You want to build up this asset throughout your job search. The more details, the better. Look at your job inventory spreadsheet like that deck of cards I mentioned in Chapter 1. Every time you add a new job to the spreadsheet, you turn over another card. The more cards that you add, the closer you get to an ace. Keep in mind, there's probably going to be a couple of jokers, too. We can't control that—LOL.

One other thing I want to mention is that your Job Inventory Spreadsheet is separate from your Job Search Journal. Your journal is to keep all your notes and exercises in one place. Your Job Inventory Spreadsheet should be an Excel document you can update electronically on a daily or weekly basis. You will, of course, want to save it for future searches. Keep your Job Inventory Spreadsheet on your desktop for easy access because you are going to revisit it regularly.

Step 3: Employee Referrals and Applications

Most people think the best job search strategy is to apply to as many positions as possible in the hopes that, eventually, someone will hire you. As I mentioned earlier in this book, that is no longer the best approach, and there are statistics to prove it. Some studies show that as little as 2% of candidates who apply for a job are selected for a job interview. *Forbes* recently reported that the average job advertised receives 118 applications, and only 20% of those will make it through to the interview stage. Please resist the urge to randomly apply to positions online. Instead, seek out employee referrals first.

An "employee referral" is simply someone at a company who is willing to present your resume to a hiring authority on your behalf. This is key to your success and will drastically improve your chances of getting to the front of the line (or at least being included in the line). According to JobVite, research shows that referred applicants are significantly more likely to be hired: five times more likely than the average applicant, and 15 times more likely than an applicant who found the position via a job posting. As many as 78% of recruiters feel that referrals are the best way to find qualified candidates, and referral hires reportedly have better job satisfaction and stay with companies longer.

Here's how this process works. Before applying to a specific position, go to LinkedIn and, in the search bar, type in the company name for the position you're interested in. See if you have any first-degree connections with someone in the organization. Perhaps you know someone, or perhaps you are connected to someone who knows someone. The whole idea is to find someone within the organization who is willing to refer your resume to a key contact internally for that specific position. (This is exactly why I wanted you to build up your LinkedIn network as much as possible. The more connections you have, the better your chances of finding someone who can help you).

When you find that person, you will ask for the referral by sending a direct message requesting that they share your resume with the hiring manager rather than submit it online (to the big black hole of resumes that exists on the internet). Statistically, applicants with such a referral get an interview 50% of the time (Source: Zippia.com). We will discuss *how* to ask for job referrals in the next chapter.

Important Note: Do not let fear win. Fear is going to try to take you out. Fear is going to try to prevent you from sending out requests to people and asking for help. You might say things to yourself like, *Well, what if they don't get back to me?* or *What if I send the request, and they tell me they're not interested?* Well, what if you send the request and they DO want to help you? You won't know unless you ask.

Fear is going to try to prevent you from doing the things that you need to do to be successful in your job search. I'm telling you now, do *not* give up! You have nothing to lose. You need to try, and you need to try on a daily, if not weekly, basis.

Applying to Jobs Without a Referral

If you have exhausted all options, tried everything, and still can't find anyone you know within an organization, it may be time to apply directly to the company. If given a choice, my advice would be to apply via email (if possible) rather than through an online application. When you apply for a position, it is important to follow the exact instructions given to you. A lot of people seem to miss the finer details. For example, if the company asks for your resume as a PDF document, don't send it as a Word doc. If they're requesting a cover letter, include it. As a best practice, do not apply multiple times to the same position or apply to several positions at the same company all at once. Internally, people keep track of those things. It will just make you look desperate.

Follow Instructions When Applying

I want to share a story about the importance of following instructions when applying for a position. A colleague of mine posted a position online recently. He received 1,150 applications and felt that most people did not actually read the job description (based on how many non-qualified applicants there were). Only 19 people bothered to answer the additional questions he asked. Of those 19 people, only one person answered the questions competently. That was the only person invited to interview, and they eventually got the job.

This is a great example of why it is so important to be thorough in your efforts and follow instructions completely. I am often asked how to stand out in a crowded pool of applicants and competitive job seekers. Sometimes, it is a matter of doing the small things and the basics really well.

Facts About Job Postings

When it comes to online job postings from companies and recruiters, what you see may not be what you get. There are several things to be aware of when it comes to opportunities found online. First, beware of "ghost posts." A ghost post is a job posting for a position that has already been filled or was created for the sole purpose of harvesting candidates for future roles. This is also known as "pipelining" candidates. Another example is when a company has already selected an internal candidate for an open position but needs to post the position externally to satisfy a corporate recruitment policy. In either case, the posting is not real or has already been filled.

I realize this concept may freak you out and sound discouraging. Please keep in mind that ghost posts account for a fraction of actual job postings, but they are a thing to be aware of. This is just one more of the unfortunate frustrations of the job search process. Not much we can do about it, but it's important to be aware.

Job Applicants

One of the greatest frustrations I hear from job seekers is that they will apply for a position and see that there are 1,792 other applicants. Yes, I made that number up to prove a point. Whatever the number is, it seems quite cruel to show the world how many people are actually vying for the same position.

That said, please understand the number you see is NOT the actual number of qualified applicants. Some websites will include the number of people who may have clicked on the button or never fully completed the application. As I mentioned earlier, the number will also include the many unqualified applicants who are applying "just in case" but who will likely never be considered.

Bottom line: pay no attention to the number of applicants listed. Run your own race and stay focused on what is in your control. Do not get discouraged or change your game plan in any way.

Should I Apply if I Am Not FULLY Qualified?

People often ask me, "What if I do not have the exact experience for the job?" or "How do I stand out to employers and get noticed?" My answer is the same for both and involves **Three Key Factors** employers consider when reviewing job applicants:

1. **Experience and Performance:** Do you have experience and expertise in this position or a similar one? How does your professional experience correlate to the responsibilities and requirements of this role? What relationships do you have that can aid you in this role, and is your network an asset to the organization? What have you accomplished? What success have you achieved? What problems have you solved? What is your track record of success, and how will it make you attractive for this specific role?

2. **Skills and Background:** What are your key transferable skills and strengths, and how do they align with those needed to succeed in this role? What professional tools are you proficient in? What are you knowledgeable or educated in, and how can the company leverage that knowledge?

3. **Attitude:** Why would someone want you on their team? What energy do you bring to an organization? How do you display positivity? Do you go the extra mile? Are you a person of integrity? Are you a team player? Are you a self-starter who shows up early and stays late?

- Factors one and two make a candidate more qualified.
- Factor number three makes a candidate more attractive and desirable.
- Attitude is not always apparent in a job application and resume, but it absolutely is in an interview.

Bonus Tip: Networking is the great equalizer in any job search. If you have the right relationships and connections, you can be less qualified but better recommended than others. Recommendations and employee referrals go a long way. I had a conversation with the president of a very large company. He is responsible for 22,000 people and a $1.2 million budget. He explained to me that when he gets a good recommendation or a referral from someone he knows, he "makes it a priority to give that person every opportunity to win the job."

Job Application Follow-Up

Timely and tactful follow-up is key. When you apply for a position, whether it's through a referral or online, a good practice is to follow up after one week of submitting your application. Draft a simple email to the person who referred you to the job or find someone internally at the organization to see if your resume was received and if there's any feedback.

I believe in tactical persistence, but be careful not to overdo it and overstep your bounds. Do not venture into the creepy zone by coming off as a stalker and just flat-out annoying people. Keep your email brief and summarize the facts. Mention the position you applied for, name drop if you can (especially if someone referred you), and bullet out a few key highlights of why you are a fit for the position. Again, be brief; you don't need a ton of detail.

"It Worked… It Totally Worked!"

I want to tell you a story of how effective the strategy outlined in this chapter can be. A friend of mine asked if I would help his son, Richard, find a job. Rich was fresh out of college and looking for a sales job in pretty much any field. Unfortunately, he had a crappy resume and didn't know how to conduct a successful search.

I shared the exact process of this book with him. We started by cleaning up his resume and then his LinkedIn profile. I then asked him to take all of the jobs he had already applied to, as well as the new jobs he wanted to pursue, and do searches on LinkedIn to see if he was connected to anyone in those organizations. I explained the rest of the process, including the importance of employee referrals, and left Rich to handle the process from there.

Several weeks went by. I heard nothing, and quite frankly, I forgot about it. One day, I got a phone call from Rich. I actually thought he was calling to ask for additional advice or to see what to do next. When I picked up the phone, here's what he said: "I got a job! It worked… it totally worked!" After I congratulated him, he went on to say he had done exactly what I'd told him to do. He found someone he knew who worked at one of the target companies, and the rest is history. Richard had zero experience and not a lot of LinkedIn connections, but all it takes is one person. One referral may be all you need.

Free Download: The Job Inventory Spreadsheet.

Scan the QR code:

Chapter 6 Summary

Job Search Process Roadmap – Navigating Your Path to Success

- Step 1: The Search
- Step 2: Job Inventory Spreadsheet
- Step 3: Employee Referrals and Applications
- Applying to Jobs Without a Referral
- Follow Instructions When Applying
- Facts About Job Postings
- Job Applicants
- Should I Apply if I Am Not FULLY Qualified?
- Job Application Follow-Up

CHAPTER 7

Networking: Building a Future for Success

If you were to ask me, "What is the single most important thing I need to do to win my dream job?" My answer would be **networking.** Networking is the most effective way to achieve job search success. According to Chris Kolmar, writing for the website Zippia.com, "80% of jobs are filled through networking. Recent research shows that the majority of jobs in the U.S. are filled through networking or personal and professional connections. In fact, according to an article published by CNBC, roughly 70% of jobs are never published publicly on job sites."

The goal of networking is to build relationships one person at a time. Relationships are essential to your job search and career. I would argue that relationships are career currency. The more relationships you have, the greater your career worth. It is important to look at your relationships as an asset you are trying to grow over time. The stronger and bigger your network, the more valuable you are to others and, most importantly, yourself.

What is Networking?

Networking is the key to job search success, career success, and personal success. The Oxford definition of networking is "the action or process of interacting with others to exchange information and develop professional or social contacts." Networking is the great equalizer in any job search process. In any group of job search candidates, some will be more qualified than others, but those with the best relationships may wind up going to the top of the list or at least be included in the search.

As I said before, applying to random positions online is not a good job search strategy. The best strategy is to grow and build your network so you can get a foot in the door and be included in the applicant pool with someone vouching for you as a candidate.

Building a Strong Network

Networking is a verb. The goal is to create new relationships every day and grow your network throughout your career. You're going to need to work at them and nurture them, and you will then create friendships that will help develop your professional network. You will get to a point where building your network may actually mean you never have to go through a job search again in the future.

What do I mean by that? When you have a really strong network, people are going to come to you to ask you if you're interested in a job they have available in their company. That's how it works. People often say to me, "Tom, I haven't had to revise my resume in five years because people in my network recruited me to come work on their team." That is the beauty of networking. Once you have an established and vast network, you have relationships you can leverage in many ways. Again, approximately 70% of jobs never get published publicly on job sites.

Warm Outreach

The best place to start your networking efforts is with people you know. My friend Mike was just laid off from a major company that cut 12,000 jobs.

He had been there for 34 years. Mike had no warning, and the severance package was a fraction of what he expected or hoped for. I learned of Mike's situation from a text message he sent to our college group of friends asking if we would keep him in mind for opportunities. There were 20 people in the text group. It was a brilliant strategy. I certainly jumped in to help. Several others had suggestions and made introductions to professional contacts and colleagues. Not only do I think his text request will help him find his next position faster, but he explained how encouraged he was after getting so much support and help from his college buddies.

Warm outreach is pretty simple: reach out to everyone you know who may be in a position to help you. This could be through text, email, phone calls, LinkedIn messaging, etc. Some will actually post on LinkedIn to explain that they are seeking work. LinkedIn also has an "Open to Work" banner you can turn on when seeking opportunities. Keep in mind that everyone can see it. If you are currently employed, it is not as easy to broadcast the message that you are open to opportunities, but if you are unemployed, I recommend any and all means to inform others. Get creative, and do not be afraid to ask. Warm outreach is a no-brainer. Make it a regular part of your weekly process.

Quick Tip: One of the best ways to stay in front of people is to send over an updated resume after a few weeks. If interaction and engagement have lagged a bit, send a simple email stating that you want to share a copy of your most updated resume. This acts as a professional reminder of your search and might stir up some activity and engagement.

What Is the Best Networking "Approach"?

The art of networking is not just about connecting but also about asking. We often hear the phrase "call to action," a marketing term that refers to encouraging a person or audience to respond. In the job search process, a call to action is a request. We are asking for something. The question is, how do you ask? As I said, do not fear. You have to take a chance.

Now, you also need to be very tactful and take the best approach. One of the first concepts I learned in sales training when I was brand new to the industry is what's called the "initial benefit statement," or IBS. The IBS is quite simple. It means that in any request, even when networking, you give the benefit to the other person.

Let me give you an example. Early in my career, I sold health insurance plans. If I called someone and said, "I'm Tom, and I want to sell you my health insurance so I can make a lot of money, buy a nice car, and live a good life," they would probably hang up the phone. But if I called the person and said, "My name is Tom, and I want to show you how you can save significant money on your health insurance each month. Can you spare five minutes of your time?" I'd have a much better chance of making a sale.

The IBS (saving the person money) is the key difference. Without the IBS, it just sounds like I am asking for a favor. I want you to do something similar in your networking, but you have to be tactful in how you do it.

Please note: the IBS comes before the call to action. Yes, I am encouraging you to include a call to action, but doing so AFTER the IBS is the key. Let me give you some examples.

LinkedIn Connection Invite: Mention a Mutual Connection

"Hi, John. I see that we're both connected to (person's name), so I wanted to see if it might benefit you if we were to connect. I would like to add you to my network and hope I can be a resource for you in the future."

The very mention of the mutual colleague's name may be enough for that person to say yes. The call to action is simply the request to connect. You also offered to be a resource to them (benefit). Another approach might be to mention something you have in common. Maybe you both went to the same school or share a similar background or skill. See if there is a mutual interest by researching them on LinkedIn. Maybe they just got a new job. If so, you can congratulate them in your request:

"Hi, [Name]. Congratulations on your new position! That's wonderful news! Best of luck to you in your new role. I wanted to see if you might be interested in connecting here on LinkedIn."

The compliment acts as a benefit as it makes them feel good, increasing the likelihood they will accept your connection request. This is the difference between sending something random and sending something that isn't very well thought out and doesn't give them a benefit. The point is, you can be successful in networking with strangers if you take the right approach.

Reciprocity

Another networking concept worth understanding is reciprocity, which is "a process of exchanging things with other people to gain a mutual benefit. The norm of reciprocity (sometimes referred to as the rule of reciprocity) is a social norm where, if someone does something for you, you then feel obligated to return the favor." (Source: Verywell Mind)

Reciprocity is actually very similar to offering a benefit statement, as the statement makes the other person want to reciprocate. It is also one of psychologist and best-selling author Robert Cialdini's seven principles of influence. Robert Cialdini is known as an expert in the science of influence. I saw him speak live, and his concept is this: do for others, and they will want to do for you. This may be something as simple as offering a compliment, congratulations, or recognition. Maybe the person just wrote an article, and you want to let them know that you appreciate their work.

Remember the story of Gary, who made himself visible through LinkedIn engagement. The reason I agreed to the informational interview with him was that I felt like I needed to reciprocate for all of the goodwill, compliments, comments, likes, etc., on LinkedIn. That's reciprocity.

What Is the Best Way to Network?

The most obvious, easiest, and best-all-around place for networking is LinkedIn. We already discussed the Daily Action Plan for LinkedIn Connections, which is a networking strategy. Let's pick things up from there. The next step is to network through direct messages and engagement.

Again, follow the strategy we learned from Gary: become relevant. Go into that person's LinkedIn feed and engage with people in the community. So, if they're engaging with a community, you're engaging with the same community. Look for other people in your dream job community and see who's most relevant.

LinkedIn is also a great place to do research and find out who you should be adding to your network and why. You're going to meet people through this engagement strategy. You are going to see other people commenting. Other people are going to see you comment. And before you know it, you're going to be very visible to others, as they are to you. You will wind up with connections just by participating in this engagement.

Seek Out Mentors

A great networking tactic and job search strategy is to find mentors, people who have already done what you want to do. They have landed their dream job, found success, and are already thriving in their career. You need to find those people and learn from them. Mimic them. Model them. Make them your advocates.

Again, I will go back to Gary's example. He started at the very beginning as a no-name. He later told me that he found six mentors in his job search. Six people agreed to mentor him and help him along the way. It is hard to say how many mentors one can expect, but I would shoot for at least three. Very often, mentors are the key to getting your foot in the door. You may actually wind up asking a mentor for a job referral. Your mentors may be pivotal to you winning your next job.

Informational Interviews

An informational interview is a meeting where you can learn about the real-life experience of someone working in your dream job. It is a networking tactic that puts you in front of potential mentors, hiring managers, and decision makers. An informational interview with someone comes before they agree to be your mentor.

Asking people for informational interviews is something you need to incorporate into your daily job search process. There are huge upsides and benefits to doing informational interviews. The key is that you need to ask. Again, do not be afraid. Do not let fear win. Respect people's time, and make sure you offer to reciprocate in some way. At the very least, be appreciative, and of course, send a thank-you email within 24 hours.

The key to informational interviews is to learn as much as you can about your dream job. At the same time, be sure to find out about how this person went about winning theirs and how they found success in their role.

Out of respect for the person's time, be prepared for the conversation. First, answer the phone with a level of excitement and expectation. One of my biggest pet peeves is when I have a set call with someone, and they answer the phone with a weak "hello," as if they were not expecting to hear from me. Next, have a good list of well-thought-out questions that show you did some homework and are prepared for the conversation. The more you impress this person, the better your chances of them offering their mentorship.

Your goal is to learn as much as you can while potentially finding mentors. The more informational interviews you do, the more knowledgeable you will become and the more mentors you will wind up with.

Beware of CREEPERS

I want to caution you about the dark side of networking. Unfortunately, there are some creepy people out there. In our office, we call them "creepers." I received a phone call from a family member who was looking to secure her first position out of college. I coached her on exactly what we have discussed in this book, including all of the networking strategies and tactics. She explained that she got a message from an alumnus at her college who was working in a similar industry. He was very nice at first and agreed to an informational interview, and nothing seemed out of place. Then he started texting her random odd questions during weird hours, questions outside the norm of a career or professional context. I advised her to block his number and remove his LinkedIn connection. Thankfully, it ended there, but it is a reminder to be cautious. If someone gets overly personal or inappropriate during networking or a professional interaction, disengage immediately and make others aware (supervisors, mentors, teammates, etc.).

Engaging With Recruiters and Headhunters

I recommend you find recruiters, also known as "headhunters," who specialize in your dream job space. The term "headhunter" is a bit dated, so I will stick to "recruiter." The best way to identify the right recruiter is to ask colleagues, friends, or industry associates. You can certainly do an Internet or LinkedIn search as well, but asking a mentor or colleague in your space is your best bet.

As you may know, I have been a specialized pharmaceutical/biotech recruiter for 25 years. My niche area of focus is in medical affairs, more specifically, medical science liaison, or MSL, recruitment. The reason I mention all this is to exemplify how niche a recruiter or recruitment firm can be.

You need to find the niche recruiters best suited to help you. They are out there. They have great clients and relationships. They will be very knowledgeable in your dream job space. They may even have podcasts or blogs. At the very least, I am sure they can guide you through the process and help educate you. Not to mention, they will hopefully have opportunities for you to consider and apply to. It is the goal of a recruiter to place you with one of their clients. The company most often pays recruiters, so it should not cost you anything to work with them unless you are hiring a specialized coach.

The best time to engage a recruiter is at the very beginning of your search or before or during your final semester of school. You want to incorporate recruiters into your job search strategy because they can be very beneficial to you, not only in your search but throughout your career, if you create the right relationships and find the right ones.

I recommend engaging with recruiters via LinkedIn. Send a personalized connection request. It should be short, polite, and to the point, not "Hey, can you find me a job?" And yes, people say that to me all the time. Use the same principles of engagement for an initial benefit statement for interactions with recruiters. Here's an example.

> "Dear Recruiter,
>
> John Doe suggested I reach out to you as I begin my job search. He mentioned that you are an expert in your field and you would be an excellent resource. I'm sure you're very busy. I was wondering if it would be okay if I could share my current resume with you and perhaps set up a brief five-minute call at your convenience if time allows. Thank you in advance."

How can someone say no to such a well-crafted request? That is a great example of an engaging and thoughtful message. I recommend you use something like it not only when you're reaching out to third-party recruiters but also as an example for when you're sending out networking and LinkedIn connection requests. This style and format work well, so consider creating a few versions and stick with the one you feel is best.

What the Candidate Should Expect From the Recruiter

First off, most recruiters are working on behalf of their clients to fill open positions. They may not necessarily only be working to place you at a company. The company typically pays for the fee for recruiters, so it should not cost you anything to work with them. The ultimate goal for everyone is for the recruiter to fill an open position for the client, ideally with you as the candidate. If the recruiter does not have any suitable positions for you to consider, that may not be the case, but if they do, expect them to represent you in the same way a sports agent represents an athlete (for lack of a better analogy).

The recruiter should help you:

- Navigate the job search process.
- Be informed about the client/company and have prior experience with them.
- Know the details about the job opening and what the hiring team is looking for.
- Know the details about the hiring manager and interview process to help you prepare.
- Inform you of the compensation ranges and expectations for the position.
- Assist with interview scheduling, preparation, and guidance.
- Assist in the job offer negotiation process.
- Answer any and all questions along the way.

What the Recruiter Should Expect From the Candidate

The most important thing recruiters look for in candidates is transparency. Being up front, honest, and responsive will make the process more effective and ensure a great relationship. Recruiters need to know the details to be in a position to help you.

- What is most important to you in your job search?
- Why are you seeking opportunities, and why would you consider leaving your current company?
- What is your timeline for starting a new position?
- How far along are you in the interview process with other companies (to be mindful of timing)?
- What are your compensation expectations or requirements?

Ask

Before I close out this chapter on networking, I want to encourage you to *ask*. Do not let fear hold you back. You aren't going to build your network unless you ask people. You are not going to get informational interviews unless you ask people. You are not going to be able to get job referrals unless you ask people.

This is a common problem that I see in the job search process. People don't take action because they're afraid to do so. If you sit on the sidelines, you're going to be left out. Don't forget: someone else out there wants the same job you do, and they will be asking for all of these things. Are you going to let that person outwork you? Remember the quote that inspired Tim Tebow: "Somewhere he is out there working while I am not, and when we meet, he will win."

Example: Networking Formula for Success

Let me tell you a quick story about Mario and his formula for success. Mario was a job seeker with no experience, looking to break into his dream job. He had a great background and a good story to tell. He also had a great resume, and he was not afraid to ask. Mario told me that throughout his search, he sent out three hundred messages to people on LinkedIn, all hiring managers, recruiters, and professionals in his dream job community. In those three hundred messages, he requested informational interviews, mentorship, and connections.

Mario's efforts resulted in over 35 conversations with influential dream job professionals, including hiring managers. He wound up with several mentors and some really great relationships. Most importantly, several of these contacts were willing to help Mario in his job search. Anytime he saw his dream job posted at one of their companies, he asked for a referral. This tactic, the same one I explained in this book, resulted in multiple interviews with several companies. Ultimately, Mario wound up with three job offers as a result of all those efforts.

I'm not a mathematician, but you can see that putting in the numbers, doing the work, and not being afraid to ask will increase your chances of getting in front of the right people so you can be selected for your dream job.

Free Download: My list of Top Resources for Professional Networking and Relationship Building.

Scan the QR code:

Chapter 7 Summary

Networking: Building a Future for Success

- What Is Networking?
- Building a Strong Network
- Warm Outreach
- What Is the Best Networking "Approach"?
- LinkedIn Connection Invite: Mention a Mutual Connection
- Reciprocity
- What Is the Best Way to Network?
- Seek Out Mentors
- Informational Interviews
- Beware of CREEPERS

- **Engaging With Recruiters and Headhunters**
    - What the Candidate Should Expect From the Recruiter
    - What the Recruiter Should Expect From the Candidate
- **Ask**
- **Example: Networking Formula for Success**

CHAPTER 8

Personal Branding, Social Media, and Engagement

What is your brand? You should already have an idea from our work in Chapters 2 and 3. We went through several exercises to determine your dream job and career identity. You identified your core values, skills, strengths, and weaknesses. You completed extensive research on your dream job and the market. This information is critical to your branding efforts, which can play a huge role in your job search success and throughout your career.

Branding

Your personal brand is your online reputation. It is your digital imprint. It can translate into your career image, so you have to work at it. What social media platforms have you adopted? What social media platforms are you active on? How active are you on LinkedIn? Does your current personal brand align with your professional brand? These are some important questions to ask yourself.

Please understand that your personal brand will seep into your professional brand. People follow and respect those they know, like, and trust. Hiring managers, recruiters, and professional colleagues will find your brand, which no longer makes it just personal. Is your personal brand currently in line with your professional brand?

How much are you working on your personal brand? Is it helping your career identity? Is it positioning you in the right way? The lack of a social brand is not a good thing. People are going to look for you, and what they find is going to determine the impression they have of you personally and professionally.

This is not to say I am suggesting you need to be on Facebook, Instagram, X, TikTok, etc. Some people prefer NOT to be on social media. That's okay, but we have already established the career importance of LinkedIn. At the very least, I encourage you to have a fully complete LinkedIn profile and recommend that you follow the instructions in this book on how to use the platform in your job search and career. So, even if you are not a social media person, let's at least agree on LinkedIn.

Let me share a story worth thinking about. I was recently involved in a senior-level job search for one of my biotech clients. The candidate pool was crowded with many qualified applicants. After a lengthy search and interview process, it came down to two final candidates. The hiring team was torn as to which applicant they wanted to move forward with. Each candidate was equally qualified. Each candidate showed the same level of interest and excitement for the position and the company. Each candidate deserved the job, and the hiring team was looking for a tiebreaker.

Confidentially, the hiring manager told me that he made his decision after checking both candidates' social media channels to see what he could find that stood out (good, bad, or otherwise). One of the two final candidates had a brand that was much more aligned with the managers' expectations and the company culture. He felt that this person's brand was more professional and inviting than the other finalists. The person who ultimately got the job was awarded the position specifically because they took the time to build up the right personal and professional brand.

As I mentioned earlier in this book, recruiters and hiring managers will visit your LinkedIn profile to see what your digital brand is. What does your photo say about you? What content do you post (if any)? What do you like, share, and comment on? Are you active in the dream job community? Are you an influencer in the community? Many find the idea of branding and social media exhausting (for lack of a better word). I get it. Branding is a lot of work. But when done correctly and consistently, it can make a huge difference in your job search and career. Most importantly, it can be the difference between you and the competition.

The Know, Like, and Trust Factor

The know, like, and trust factor, or KLT factor (or principle), is a marketing concept focused on the benefits of people knowing, liking, and trusting you. It is a commonly used term that relates to social efforts for branding and influence. While often used as an effective sales strategy, incorporating the KLT factor into your job search is a very good idea.

I will refer to the KLT factor in our discussions on branding and networking as a recommended strategy for creating influence and building relationships. It is a pretty simple concept when you think about it. We want people to know us, like us, and trust us. When we establish KLT, we create influence, build our brand, and establish our network, which is crucial to our career development and progression.

Content Strategy

What is the best system or formula for the creation of content? How can you make sure you are enforcing your career image? What is the best way to promote your brand through content? I'm going to share a simple concept that will help you with your content creation. I call it "The five E's" of social content:

1. **Educate:** Offer content that teaches people something.
2. **Encourage:** Create content that inspires, motivates, and brings courage to others.
3. **Entertain:** Make sure your content is enjoyable.
4. **Engage:** Try to engage visitors with the content you produce.
5. **Emotion:** Make people feel something through your content. Create positive emotion.

To be clear, you do not need to incorporate all five E's into every piece of content. The goal is to use the five E's as a guide for what and how you create your content. For example, when you're looking to create a post on LinkedIn or other social media platforms, think about how this content might educate someone. Is it encouraging? Would it entertain someone?

Then ask yourself, *What could I say in this content that will engage the audience?* Perhaps you can end with a question or call to action. You might also ask yourself, *Am I creating emotion through this? Am I making people feel something when they see this message, this image, this post, this quote?* Ask yourself these questions before you click the "post" or enter button.

Creating and sharing content that educates, encourages, entertains, engages, and creates emotion in others will help you build a great personal and professional brand.

Value-Based Content

When creating content for a job search and career development, it's crucial to focus on value, not vanity. Rather than chasing likes and adding random followers, create content that has value. You want to tell stories that have meaning and are relevant to the community. The word "relevant" is very important because it relates to what the individual finds valuable for their dream job, career, and community.

You want to stay positive and inspiring so others find motivation and encouragement by following you. Your content should embody the qualities and attributes of those who succeed in your dream job. You will find that people will respect and want to follow you when you offer value.

Content Ideas

One of the biggest challenges is finding great content ideas and strategies. People often tell me that they are stuck on what it is they want to share and what type of content they want to produce. Quite frankly, posting a lot of "me too" content (repurposing and recreating something that someone else has already done) comes off as inauthentic. As a result, it's much less effective. So, how can you be authentic and share content that other people will appreciate?

Here are some ideas:

- **Share career milestones.** This means you have to constantly pay attention to different things happening in your career each day and then decide what you feel is worth sharing with others.

- **Share wins.** Your own wins and maybe others' wins. Everyone loves a winner. Try to find content ideas that showcase people winning.

- **Share lessons and challenges.** Sometimes, it makes sense to get real. When you see someone confronting a challenge or when you have learned a lesson from someone, share the story or lesson tactfully. Of course, don't mention names. Be careful to maintain confidentiality and privacy. However, sharing lessons and challenges is a way to provide momentum and results.

- **Share how you got results.** Often, people create content that comes off as bragging. That's not what I'm asking you to do. However, if you can showcase ways you have found success and how others have achieved, gained, or found momentum and progress, it will be very beneficial to your audience.

- **Post how-to content.** Perhaps you're an expert in something or just found out a really good way to do something. Share it. Be creative. Show things that you want to use yourself or that you learned from others, and create a how-to post about it. This is a great way to engage your audience.

- **Poll others.** Get people involved. Creating polls on LinkedIn is a great way to establish an audience and get engagement from a community. Don't worry about how many people participate because, over time, more and more people will appreciate the polls that you put out. As long as your polls are in line with the dream job community, they can benefit from the information that comes from them.

- **Share other people's content**. There are going to be people you like, value, and respect in your community and your LinkedIn network. Those people, I am sure, will be very happy to see you sharing their content. It's just a matter of reposting, either with or without comments, to share value with others but also to show appreciation for people in your network who are creating and sharing value. Consider sharing other people's content on a weekly basis, but do not make this your only content strategy. This is also a great example of reciprocity. Help others, and they will want to help you.

- **Share quotes that inspire.** This is easy content. When you come across a quote that resonates with you and inspires you, it's very simple to create a quick post. You can put it on any of the social platforms, and I'm sure it will resonate with others. Just be sure to cite or credit the person responsible for the quote.

- **Be authentic.** Find ways to create content that shows your authentic self. Be true to your brand, be true to yourself, and be creative. But be careful not to get overly personal or overshare. Try to stay away from politics and strong opinions. Avoid negativity and divisive ideology. I often see people get super personal, which changes the brand of the individual personally and professionally. Authenticity is good. Oversharing is not.

Content Consistency

As important as it is to produce quality, value-based content, it is equally important to be consistent. Top influencers and branding experts have content calendars and posting schedules that ensure consistency. Even if you are just getting started in your branding efforts, creating a set schedule of how many times per week, what types of content, and on what platforms you post is a great way to find your own level of consistency.

Don't overthink it. Develop a strategy, commit to it on a calendar based on what you are capable of producing, and give it a try. Very often, the content you think will elicit the best response is sometimes outdone by content you did not expect to hit. Trying different things and sticking to a schedule will help establish your branding plans.

Engagement Strategy

Engagement equals visibility. If you want to be found, you have to be seen, and the more you engage with your community, the more visible you will be. I already used the example of Gary and how he found his dream job.

I can tell you Gary was one of the most visible people I saw in the dream job community until he landed his desired role.

You need to be seen by those in your dream job space to become relevant. That's what engagement is all about: liking, sharing, commenting, congratulating, and being active with those in the dream job space. This is not a difficult thing to do; it just requires daily action.

I recommend that you engage with your dream job community on a daily basis, even if it's only for 15 minutes. It's actually a great way to unwind at the end of the day because it's super easy. It doesn't require a whole lot of effort, but it's incredibly impactful.

Here's a quick engagement exercise:

Engagement for Visibility

- Go to 10 different influencer accounts or hashtags and comment on each.
- Respond to 10 commenters on those accounts.
- Go to 10 of your ideal contacts and comment on their accounts.

START CALLOUT BOX

Free Download: My Branding Strategy Article: "The New Social Currency."

Scan the QR code:

Chapter 8 Summary

Personal Branding, Social Media, and Engagement

- Branding: What Is Your Personal Brand
- Know, Like, and Trust Factor
- Content Strategy
- Value-Based Content
- Content Ideas
- Content Consistency
- Engagement Strategy
- Engagement for Visibility

CHAPTER 9

The Interview: How You WIN the Job
PART 1: Planning and Practice

Interviews are the most crucial part of the job search process. While the ultimate goal is to win your dream job, the near-term goal is to get interviews. The more interviews you do, the better chance you have of getting an offer or even multiple offers. Every interview gives you the opportunity to improve. You will also get a chance to meet new people in your dream job industry. You're developing new relationships and LinkedIn connections, and you are growing your network within your dream job community. The only downside to interviewing is the time commitment.

The interview process has four phases:

1. **Planning and Research**
2. **Practice**
3. **Performance**
4. **Follow up**

Since these four phases of the interview process are so crucial, I broke this chapter into two parts. Let's start with the two phases that happen prior to the interview.

1) PLANNING AND RESEARCH

I will argue that the MOST important part of the interview process is the planning and research. Before you even start the interview preparation process, you must know how much time you are able to commit each day or each week to the prep work. You need to map out a plan using your calendar and chunking your time each day.

"Chunking your time" means allocating blocks of time to specific tasks on a daily or weekly basis. For example, you might commit 30 minutes each morning, from 7:30 a.m. to 8:00 a.m., and one hour each evening, from 7:30 p.m. to 8:30 p.m., to doing the prep work. Those are chunks of time. It's very important to plan your interview prep time in small increments rather than trying to tackle it all at once. I see many people put things off till the weekend and then try to cram all their efforts into one or two days. However, if that is all you are able to commit to, do your best to be organized and make the best use of your time.

Research

You must start your preparation by researching the company. I mentioned a story earlier from my friend and hiring manager, Paul. One of the two questions he asks in every interview is: "What do you know about our company, and why would you want to work here?"

Paul told me, "Tom, when I ask what a candidate knows about the company, I don't even really care what the answer is. What I want to know is whether the person took the time to do the research or not. I'm not so much concerned about exactly what they learned, but the effort that they put into learning it."

That said, I do think it's important to do significant research on the company during your preparation, not just to win the interview but to learn everything you can about the organization to determine your true interest in the opportunity.

Here are some of the things I advise doing:

Research the Company Website

News: Start with "News" and review the latest press releases to see if there is anything you may need to be aware of or potentially discuss in the interview. You need to find out what is currently going on in the organization. Is there good news that just happened? Is there bad news that just happened? Has the earnings report just been released, or is there financial news you should be aware of? Do not get caught off guard by going into an interview and not understanding the state of affairs with the company.

Core Values: You should also look for the company's core values and see if they are listed on the website. That's often in the "About" section or someplace near "Careers" or "Culture." When you identify their core values, you will want to mention them during the interview so you can demonstrate that you want to be a part of the culture. Companies want to know that job seekers are aligned with their values and will fit in. If you can show that you agree with their core values and are excited about joining for that reason, it will definitely help your chances. You should be clear on your personal core values from our exercise in Chapter 2, so the above strategy should be easy for you.

Products/Services: Find out all of the specifics of the company's products, services, what they do, why they do it, and how they do it. Be as detailed as you can, but realize you're only able to offer a certain amount of information in interviews. So, take good notes and make sure you're ready to answer questions when they come up.

Interview Team: You will want to research the people you will be interviewing with. Thanks to LinkedIn, it should be easy to get information on all the people interviewing you. Just go to their LinkedIn profile and look at their background. See where they went to school. See if there's anything you have in common. Find out if you have any of the same or similar interests. Perhaps you share mutual connections and contacts. This information is very important because it can provide talking points and conversation starters you can bring up in the interview to show your common interests and how you are alike.

Job Description: Review and dissect the job description in detail, every word of it. Make sure you do that right before you go into the interview. You want to make sure that the information is fresh in your mind so you can explain why you're a good fit for the position. You will not be able to do that unless you have the details at the top of your mind. Be prepared to discuss how your skills and experience match the responsibilities and requirements indicated in the position. Be a storyteller. Prepare several examples of your work and tell compelling stories that show how you have succeeded in your current or prior roles that will translate to success for the company.

Virtual (Video) Interview Preparation

At the very beginning of your search, you will also need to start the preparation process for virtual interviews. In 2023, 69% of employers are incorporating video interviews into their hiring process (Source: StandoutCV). A virtual interview is one done at a remote location via Zoom, MS Teams, Google Meet, Webex or one of the other video conferencing platforms with hiring managers and company leaders.

Some of the biggest mistakes I see in interviewing right now happen with virtual interviews. People don't seem to take them seriously. They fail to prepare and do not stage their background (what the interviewer will see in the video). People don't test their equipment and often have technical issues the day of the interview. It is important to make sure your microphone and camera work properly, which means you should do a test run prior to any live interaction.

I also advise that you dress professionally. You should wear the same attire you would in a live, onsite interview. Just because the interview is virtual and you are likely in your own home, it does not mean it is casual. I recently heard of someone who showed up for a virtual interview in a T-shirt and jeans. It really upset the hiring manager and derailed the entire interview. Clearly, that was not what we advised. This person just thought, *Well, it's a virtual interview, so it's probably more casual.* I had another hiring manager tell me recently, "The candidate looked like he just got done mowing his lawn." Let me be clear about this: virtual interviews are NOT casual—It's an interview! It is important to dress properly for it.

Phone Interviews

Since the rise in popularity of video interviews, phone interviews have become less common. However, you may be asked to conduct a phone interview, commonly called a "phone screen."

Please be aware that a phone interview is NOT just an information-gathering session; it's the real deal. People who don't take phone interviews seriously may not see another step. It's as important as every other part of the interview process. You will be judged on how you answer the phone, how you say goodbye, and everything in between. There's a 100% chance you will be judged on how much interest and enthusiasm you show for the position. I cannot stress this enough. Phone interviews are often where you make the first impression.

I made a statement earlier, and I'm going to say it again: when all things are equal amongst candidates in a job search, the position is always awarded to the candidate who shows they want the job the most. This goes for phone, virtual/video, and live onsite interviews. People often ask me, "How can I express interest in a phone interview?" One way is to ask good questions. Select questions that show you did your homework and came prepared. Choose questions about the position and its responsibilities that only someone who wants the job would ask.

2) PRACTICE

"Proper preparation prevents poor performance," known as the five P's, is a famous quote from former Secretary of State James Baker and perfect for describing interview preparation. Again, chunking time to practice before your interview is critical to your success. I recommend you anticipate questions for each interview and practice the answers. You can do this alone, in your head or in front of a mirror. You can also do it out loud in your car or in front of others. It's strictly up to you. The idea, though, is you need to practice. You need to visualize. You need to give yourself some time before interviews to get yourself ready.

Before you start, I would like to share a very important tip. When you practice, keep your answers to no more than 60 to 90 seconds. When you're asked a question in an interview, imagine there is a stopwatch running. If your response is less than 30 seconds, you may not be providing enough information (depending on the question). If it is two minutes or more, it's probably too long. I would say 45 to 60 seconds is the sweet spot.

Over-Rehearsed

One of the common byproducts of pre-interview practice is sounding overly rehearsed. This is common but not ideal. The goal is to come off as natural and genuine in your responses. Make it a part of your practice to be as natural as you can. Yes, you are practicing in your practice. Delivering an overly rehearsed answer that does not sound genuine will make you seem less authentic. More importantly, when you are natural and smooth in your delivery, it will help you crush your competition.

Questions to Be Prepared For

"Tell me about yourself." This is, perhaps, the number one interview question (probably of all time). How should you answer? The best way is to remember three words: WHO… WHAT… WHY. Start with WHO you are (career identity) and WHO you serve. Second, WHAT is your value proposition, and WHAT makes you a great fit for the dream job you are interviewing for? Third, explain WHY you are a fit and WHY you are interested in the position/company. The answer to this question may often be longer than it should be since people tend to overshare personal info. There is no reason this needs to be longer than any other question, so be careful not to offer too much detail. If you are well organized and practiced, this will be a piece of cake. Just remember, the purpose of this question is for a brief introduction about who you are professionally. If you ramble, it will start the interview off on a bad note, so practice this until you get it perfect.

Here is an example:

One: WHO are you (Career Identity), and WHO do you serve?

"I live in New Jersey, and after completing my Doctorate of Pharmacy from Rutgers University, I have spent the last eight years as a clinical pharmacist, most recently at [XYZ] Hospital. I truly enjoy caring for oncology patients as well as working in a team environment."

Two: WHAT is your value proposition?

"My entire career so far has been in oncology, and I have a passion for improving outcomes for cancer patients. I love scientific engagement and interactions with healthcare professionals to help solve their complex patient problems."

Three: WHY are you a fit, and WHY do you want the job?

"Upon reviewing the job description, I feel the combination of my background in oncology and my expertise in communicating scientific information makes me a great fit for this role. The more I learn about the organization, the more interested and excited I am about this opportunity."

Here is what it sounds like when the three parts are combined:

Tell me about yourself.

"Sure… I live in New Jersey, and after completing my Doctorate of Pharmacy from Rutgers University, I have spent the last eight years as a clinical pharmacist, most recently at [XYZ] Hospital. I truly enjoy caring for oncology patients as well as working in a team environment. My entire career so far has been in oncology, and I have a passion for improving outcomes for cancer patients. I love scientific engagement and interactions with healthcare professionals to help solve their complex patient problems. Upon reviewing the job description, I feel the combination of my background in oncology and my expertise in communicating scientific information makes me a great fit for this role. The more I learn about the organization, the more interested and excited I am about this opportunity."

"Why do you want to leave your current company?" This is another question I would expect, and certainly practice your answer to it. Keep in mind, this question is not a trick question, but it can be a trap. The reason for this is that people will often take the opportunity to get very negative about their current company. That's the trap. You want to give a reason why you're leaving but don't bash your current employer. It's unprofessional and will cast you in a poor light. Being negative about your current company will give the impression you're going to do the same thing in the future, maybe about them and their organization.

Be careful about what you offer as a reason for why you are looking to leave. Resist the urge to say, "I am not satisfied in my current role," or "I am looking for a better challenge." It just sounds "I" and disingenuous. Instead, consider something like:

"I am looking for opportunities to advance my career."

"I want to be part of a growing team that is building something."

"I want an opportunity to (mention something specific to the job description that you want to do and are qualified to do)."

Always try to relate your interests with those of the company you're applying to, especially the job description. Remember, it is very important to make potential employers think that you're not running *from* something. You're running *to* something.

"What are your greatest strengths?" You should know the answer to this question from the exercise in Chapter 2. One of the reasons we did that exercise is that I anticipate you're going to get asked this question in an interview. Just realize that you may not have one set answer to this question; you will need to tailor your answer for each interview and company. Here is why.

The best way to prepare your answer is to review the job description to get a sense of what strengths the company expects the ideal candidate to have. Compare your strengths with what the job description is looking for, and there's your answer. Think about your UVP, what makes you valuable. How are your transferable skills best aligned with the responsibilities and requirements for the position? That should guide your answer. Tell them why your strengths make you the best option for this position. Make sure you practice this answer with the job description in mind.

"What are your weaknesses?" It is quite likely you will get this question if you have already been asked about your strengths. Just think: what areas do you need to improve upon? What did you learn from the exercise in Chapter 2?

People ask me all the time, "Tom, how do I answer that question?" I can tell you what not to do. I don't think you should try to find something that's actually "a positive" and try to make it sound like a weakness. For example, people like to say, "I'm a perfectionist, and that can be a weakness because I'm never satisfied and always hard on myself." This positive-negative approach is really a non-answer and only frustrates the person asking it. The hiring manager never learns anything unless you come up with something honest but not incriminating.

I would say, "I have the tendency to be a little long-winded, and I'm not as direct as I need to be in my communication. But I am aware of it and work to control it." Then I would show the manager during the interview that I can be direct and control myself. So, ultimately, it never really develops as a real weakness because I prove myself in the interview.

Just be careful not to give them a weakness that may prevent you from getting the job. You must be able to share a real weakness without disqualifying yourself by showing you may not be able to perform key requirements and responsibilities to excel in the role.

Interview Practice (Exercise)

Make a list of potential interview questions and practice. Feel free to ask friends, use the internet, or take advantage of the free download below. The key is to practice. Take one question at a time and visualize and practice your answer while being mindful of the time. Go through all the questions rather than practicing the same one 10 times in a row. The reason is to train your brain to be able to go from question to question, which is what will happen in the interview.

My All-Time Favorite Response to an Interview Question

We were looking to hire a summer intern to help us with our social media and content creation. We had several qualified applicants who looked really good on paper. While interviewing one of the potential candidates, I asked the simple and obvious question, "Why are you interested in working with us?"

His answer: "I'm not. My mom told me I needed to get a job for the summer, and that is the only reason I am here."

Well, I really have to hand it to the kid; he was certainly honest.

Behavioral Interview Questions

It is common for employers to ask you questions like, "Tell me about a time when…" or "Describe a situation where…" These are behavioral interview questions. The purpose is for employers to learn how you handled past experiences. They also want to see how good you are at telling stories and answering questions. These questions can be very challenging to answer. It is common for people to wind up rambling when they are asked, so it is very important to learn how to handle them.

The best way to prepare for behavioral questions is to use what's called the STAR technique. This is a very common strategy. You can certainly find it on the internet; It's not a secret. STAR stands for Situation, Task, Action, Result. That's how you need to structure your answers to these questions. The STAR method forces clear and concise answers. You need to be specific, not ramble or get caught up in details. Your goal of 60- to 90-second answers does not change.

The best way to prepare for behavioral interview questions is to think about and prepare **three success stories** you've had over your career. Think about what the situation was and what action you took, and then share the result. The reason you should have three examples of success is that it is likely you will be asked a behavioral question about how you found success at something. When you get the question, tailor one of the three examples to the specific question using the STAR technique. It sounds more complicated than it is. When you can tell stories in this format, it will make it so much easier for you.

The very next thing I want you to do is think about and prepare **three challenges or setbacks** you've had in your career. It is common to get questions on how you overcame an obstacle, challenge, difficult co-worker, or trouble with a supervisor. Have the three examples of overcoming challenges prepared so you can insert them into the interview when needed.

Behavioral Interview Questions (Exercise)

Make a list of potential behavioral interview questions and practice each one. Again, you should have prepared three success stories and three challenges to help you answer those questions.

Free Download: Sample Cover Letter.

Scan the QR code:

Chapter 9 Summary

The Interview: How You WIN the Job (PART1)

- Planning and Research
    - Virtual Interview Preparation
    - Phone Interviews
    - Research
    - Company Website
    - News, Core Values
    - Products/Services
    - Interview Team
    - Job Description
    - Practice
    - Over-Rehearsed
- Questions to Prepare For
    - "Tell me about yourself."
    - "Why do you want to leave your current company?"
    - "What are your greatest strengths?"
    - "What are your weaknesses?"
    - Interview Practice (Exercise)
    - Behavioral Interview Questions (and Exercise)

CHAPTER 10

The Interview: How You WIN the Job
PART 2: Performance and Follow-up

People often ask me, what is the most important phase of the interview process? Is it the preparation and practice? Is it the performance and follow up? Let me be clear that each of the four phases of the interview process should be taken equally as serious and important. Any lapse or lack of effort in any one area can prove disastrous. That said, it all happens on game day. Practice is great, but the game is won on the field.

3) PERFORMANCE

What does it take to outperform others in an interview? Before we discuss the many ways you can crush your competition in your next interview, I want to share a story. I recently had a conversation with a colleague named Ronald, who is a hiring manager at a biotech company. Ron is in the process of hiring a new employee, so I asked him how the interviews were going. He was very frustrated. Ronald said, "At least 80 to 90% of the job candidates failed in the interview."

So, I asked, "What is it about those 80% to 90% that's so frustrating, and how did they fail?"

He said, "Here's what I'm seeing, Tom. Lack of preparation, entitlement, poor communication skills, little to no interest in the job or the company, and unsightly appearance."

He repeated that at least 80% of the time, people exemplified those attributes.

Then I asked him, "What are the other 10 to 20% doing?"

He said, "The best candidates are sharp and prepared. They dress the part and ask good questions. They're engaged, interested, and have good communication skills. They know everything there is to know about the company and the job; they clearly do their homework. They're friendly. They smile and make good eye contact. They're engaging. They check every box."

While I am not surprised by the differences between the top candidates vs. the failed candidates, I am surprised by the percentages. I would have never guessed that so many candidates would have performed so poorly with such unprofessional behavior.

Interest and Enthusiasm

I cannot stress enough the importance of showing interest in an interview. I know I've talked about it countless times. I just mentioned it in the prior story with the hiring manager, and I'm going to say it again. If you're not truly interested in the job or the company, don't bother interviewing. Ask yourself if you really want the job. Do you have a burning desire to do that job?

If you're going to the interview just for practice, you're wasting your time, and you're wasting other people's time. Yes, it is good to practice, but you don't want to waste other people's time doing it. Only pursue the positions you're genuinely interested in, and make sure you actually prepare for your interactions. Prepare to show your interest. Prepare to be excited. And if you can't do that because it's too hard, you're probably not that interested.

Don't Bring Your Mom to the Interview

Yes, you heard that right. Do NOT bring your mom or dad to the interview. We recently got a call from a hiring manager informing us that our candidate brought his mom to the interview. He was so excited and interested in the job that he wanted to do whatever he could to impress the manager. Apparently, his family was from the same part of Chile as the hiring manager. The interview was actually interrupted by the candidate's mom sharing recipes and name-dropping rather than giving her son the floor to win over the hiring team. As you can imagine, this caused quite a distraction and derailed the entire process.

As wacky as this sounds, it is not an isolated incident. I often get phone calls from parents calling on behalf of their kids who are in the job market. Mom and Dad—please don't. I know you are just trying to broker an introduction and help your kid out, but the entire idea is for the hiring authorities to see what the job seeker is capable of. If they are not capable of making a phone call or sending an email, they may not be qualified or ready for the job.

First Impression

Research has shown that people can make a first impression within seven seconds. Thirty-three percent of hiring managers claimed they knew within the first 90 seconds of an interview whether they wanted to hire that person. A first impression has four elements. Your smile, eye contact, simple gestures, and postures will immediately determine how warm and inviting you are and how comfortable you make other people feel. It is very important to be mindful of the impression you make in an interview (live or virtual).

Now we're going to talk about some of the nonverbal communication skills you need to adopt to make a strong first impression.

Interview Mode

It is important to remember that when you go into an interview, you will be judged every second throughout the entire process. You are going to be judged on how you look, what you say, and how you act. I call this **interview mode**. You need to stay 100% professional and in interview mode the entire time. Never let your guard down.

Hiring managers sometimes try to lull the candidate into a false sense of security and comfort so they will let their guard down. They want to see if the person has the tendency to get too comfortable or if they have trouble staying professional. I want to make you aware of this since this is more common than you think. If you don't expect it, you may fall into that trap.

Don't Bring Your Dog to the Interview

Yes, you heard that right. Don't bring your dog to the interview. We had a candidate who was in the final interview and a top contender for a senior-level position we were working for a client. During the Zoom interview, he brought his Goldendoodle over to show the hiring manager.

As I mentioned, sometimes, the interview panel can appear to be informal and chatty. This does not mean you should break out of interview mode. Dogs are not a part of the interview process. Even dog lovers don't want to see your dog during a professional meeting. Stay professional at all times and stay focused on winning each encounter vs. getting creative or taking risks.

Nonverbal Communication

According to Albert Mehrabian, professor emeritus of psychology at the University of California, Los Angeles, 93% of communication is nonverbal. Mehrabian is best known for his 7-38-55 model of communication. Although highly disputed, Mehrabian says that when meeting new people, the impact is 7% from what we actually say, 38% from the quality of our voice, grammar, and overall confidence, and 55% from the way we dress, act, and walk through the door. So, just think about how important nonverbal communication is in an interview process.

I shared the story of Ronald, the hiring manager who mentioned his recent interview frustrations and failures. Many of the job candidate failures included several nonverbal behaviors.

According to a nationwide survey conducted by The Harris Poll on behalf of CareerBuilder, among more than 2,100 hiring and human resource managers polled, 49 percent of employers know within the first five minutes of an interview if a candidate is a good fit for a position. By minute 15, that number reaches 90 percent. The study also found the 10 most common nonverbal mistakes made on job interviews are:

1. Failing to make eye contact: 65 percent.
2. Failing to smile: 36 percent.
3. Playing with something on the table: 33 percent.
4. Having bad posture: 30 percent.
5. Fidgeting too much in their seat: 29 percent.
6. Crossing their arms over their chest: 26 percent.
7. Playing with their hair or touching their face: 25 percent.
8. Having a weak handshake: 22 percent.
9. Using too many hand gestures: 11 percent.
10. Having a handshake that is too strong: 7 percent.

Additionally, 65% of hiring managers said clothes could be the deciding factor between two similar candidates (Source: SeedScientific).

Some of these nonverbal claims and statistics may seem a little hard to believe and are often disputed. That said, when I interview people, I learn a lot from their nonverbal behaviors and actions. I consistently hear the same from my clients and colleagues who are hiring authorities as well. Candidates spend so much time on what they want to say that they often miss other critical factors of engagement that can make or break the interview.

Importance of Eye Contact

Research shows that eye contact results in the production of the hormone oxytocin, the chemical foundation for trust. Holding eye contact with others evokes feelings of trust, respect, and alliance. To be effective, your gaze should meet the other person 60% to 70% of the time, especially in the first two seconds of an interaction. Maintaining eye contact at or less than one-third of the interaction has been shown to create a lack of trust (Source: Science of People).

I can tell you that this is a very common mistake I see people make in interviews. Job candidates often fail to make eye contact, whether in a live or virtual interview. Lack of eye contact makes the person come off as nervous, unprofessional, and lacking interest. It makes the person look shifty. Be mindful of where your eyes go. One trick is to try to see your reflection in the other person's eyes. That will ensure a proper gaze.

My wife told me another tip. When she was very young, she was afraid to look people in the eye, but her father stressed how important this was. She chose to stare at the space directly between the person's eyes, above their nose. It worked like a charm because no one knew, but it spared her the awkwardness until she matured. This may be worth a try.

Importance of Asking Questions in an Interview

One of the most overlooked yet critical parts of the interview is the questions you ask (or fail to ask). There are several reasons why this is so important:

1. You should have some genuine curiosity for certain aspects of the job and company to determine if they are a good fit for you.
2. Asking good questions shows the hiring manager you are truly interested.
3. The information you gather during the interview is important for how you handle the rest of the process, including the offer negotiation.
4. Failing to ask questions or asking the wrong questions could prove fatal. Not asking questions just comes off as a lack of interest. It can also be considered unprofessional.

Interview Questions to Ask

During your preparation, you should make a list of questions to ask during the interview. My advice is to think of questions that will help you understand whether you would be successful and happy in the role. Second, think of questions that show the hiring manager how much you are interested in working for the company and being an asset to their team. In summary, ask questions that help to see if *they* are a good fit for you and questions to see if *you* are a good fit for them.

The timing of your questions is important as well. Questions to avoid in initial interviews would be anything about benefits, vacation time, and compensation since it may just be too early to ask. You do not want to give a hiring manager the impression that you are only in it for the money and benefits. Make it about the job, the company, and the opportunity. There should be time later in the interview process for those questions. If you learn in advance that there is only one interview, you may want to learn as much as you can in that meeting. Otherwise, compensation and benefits should be discussed towards the end of the process.

The Number-One Question to Ask in an Interview

What I am about to share is not just a question but an interview strategy. I am often asked what the most important question to ask in an interview is. Ask this, "How would you describe the ideal candidate for this position?" Let the hiring manager tell you exactly what it is that they are looking for in the ideal candidate. Be sure to take good notes. Now you just learned exactly what skills, experience, and traits are most important for you to focus on for the rest of the interview. I would even be prepared to end the interview by using this info as you are thanking them for their time. It may sound like this:

> *"I can't thank you enough for this opportunity to interview with you today. And I just want to express my continued interest in this role. I think I am a great fit for this position because..." (Then repeat some of the key skills, attributes, and experience mentioned earlier, but of course, make it specific to you and in your own words.)*

Maybe it shows your strengths, your transferable skills, and your unique value proposition. Don't repeat what was said word for word because they will figure out your strategy. Quite frankly, even if they figure out the tactic you just used, I have seen hiring managers be impressed by it. I would just be sure, as always, that you can fully support any claims you make.

How to Stand Out in an Interview

The best way to stand out in an interview is to *make people like you*. Here are the best ways to do that:

1. **Listen.** Be a good listener. The more you let others speak, the better they will like you. Of course, in an interview, you will be expected to do your share of talking. The idea here is to keep your answers concise, ask good questions, and be a good listener.

2. **It's not about you.** Never make the interview all about you. What can you do for me? Why should I work for you? You want to make it about them. Show how you can be valuable to the manager and the organization. Yes, interviews are a two-way street. However, to stand out, show how you can be an asset to them while deciding for yourself if they are the right fit or not.

3. **Similarity Attraction Effect.** We like people who are like us. Try to find things that you have in common with the hiring manager and the people you are interviewing with. Find a connection. When you do your research on LinkedIn, try to find mutual connections. It's great if you can name-drop or at least show some type of commonality with the person you're interviewing with. Perhaps there's a school, sport, or something else you can find out about that person that shows how you are connected.

4. **Evoke Emotion.** "We are always making people feel something." This is a quote I hear often from my coach, Ed Mylett. Be mindful of how you make others feel. You want others to feel your passion, interest, and energy. You want each interviewer to say, "Wow, I got a really good feeling about that person." That's what it means to evoke emotion.

Common Interest Story

I had a candidate named Manish who was in an interview that, in his opinion, was not going well. He said that the hiring manager was as cold as ice—completely emotionless. The manager clearly did not want to conduct this interview or was just having a bad day. Manish felt that the only way he could revive this conversation was to find something to pique this person's interest. He looked around the room to see if there was a photo or personal artifact that would indicate a hobby of some sort. Nothing. He noticed that the interviewer was also of Indian descent, so he thought he would take a chance and said, "While growing up in Bangladesh…"

At that point, the Interviewer's expression changed visibly. His eyes perked up, and he said, "You were born in Bangladesh? I was born in Bangladesh! What town are you from?" Manish mentioned the town and learned that the interviewer was from the same place (which is a very small town and an interesting coincidence). The interviewer asked, "What school did you go to?" As you guessed it, Manish went to the same school as the interviewer. Needless to say, five words, "while growing up in Bangladesh," changed the entire course of the interview.

Granted, this may not be a likely scenario for you in your next interview. However, the point is to seek common interests. More importantly, take a chance if you can. Mention something you may have in common or reference something of interest to the other person using visual cues in the office or information from research.

4) FOLLOW-UP

The last part of the interview process, which can sometimes get lost or forgotten, is the follow-up. I cannot stress enough the importance of following up on each interview. It's actually very simple: you just email a thank-you note within 24 hours. My advice is to send a note to each interviewer separately as opposed to sending the same message to all interviewers. Sending individualized thank-you notes is a great way to go the extra mile. Maybe reference something that you discussed specifically in the interview that will make the person remember you in a way that gives them a good feeling. Perhaps it will make them want to move you forward in the process.

The follow-up is an incredibly important part of the process because it is expected. If you fail to send a thank-you, the process may be over as a result. I recently had a situation where a hiring manager was trying to decide among candidates. He ranked the candidates in order, and one of the criteria he used was thank-you notes, not just who sent them and who didn't, but the quality of each. He also looked at the amount of time it took for each person to follow up and how individualized the notes were. This is a great example of just how important thank-you notes and follow-ups are.

Do not let a failure to follow up be your downfall. Following up is within our control, so be sure to make it a part of your process.

What Is Ghosting?

So, you completed the interview process and sent out your thank-you notes and a week has gone by, but you have not heard a peep. You do not know where you stand, and now you are anxious. What do you do next?

I suggest you send an email to your recruiter (if you are working with one) or the talent acquisition (HR) contact at the company, a short and simple message to express continued interest and inquire about the expected time frame for a decision from the hiring team. There is a good chance you may have completed your interview process before other candidates have finished their pre-scheduled interviews. In this case, the team will need to complete all interviews before coming to a consensus on which candidate will be selected for the position. The silence and lack of communication is often called **ghosting**.

Job seekers may feel ghosted by companies and even recruiters when long periods go by without updates or communication. A logical explanation is that there is no news to report. The search is still in process. Another explanation may be that the search is over; they selected another candidate, and no one told you. I certainly hope that does not happen to you.

My advice is to take matters into your own hands and tactfully follow up in respectable time frames. I would even ask your recruiter or HR contact what might be a good time to check back again. That way, there is a mutually agreed cadence of communication, and you can prevent the dreaded feeling of being ghosted. Keep in mind that some recent studies show the average time for employers to contact candidates after an interview is 12 days. In some countries, 1 in 10 employers will take longer than one month to give feedback to candidates. Research also suggests that it could take three weeks for an official job offer to be made in writing from the day of the final interview.

START CALLOUT BOX

Free Download: Interview Tracking Spreadsheet.

Scan the QR code:

Chapter 10 Summary

The Interview: How You WIN the Job (PART 2)

- Performance
    - Interest and Enthusiasm
    - Don't Bring Your Mom to the Interview
    - First Impression
    - Interview Mode
    - Don't Bring Your Dog to the Interview
    - Nonverbal Communication
    - Importance of Eye Contact
    - Importance of Asking Questions in an Interview
    - Interview Questions to Ask
    - The Number-One Question to Ask in an Interview
    - How to Stand Out in an Interview
- Follow-Up
    - The Importance of Thank-You Notes
    - What Is Ghosting?

CHAPTER 11

Negotiate Your Way to Success

Of course, the ultimate goal of your job search is to win your dream job. The final step in the process is preparing for and negotiating the job offer. Negotiating a job offer can be tricky – and disastrous if not handled properly. Proper negotiation is important to ensure you get the best offer possible while staying tactful and professional. It is never good to upset your future employer and start on a bad note, or worse, over-negotiate and lose the offer altogether. Yes, that can happen. More on that later. The best way to explain the job offer negotiation process is to break it down into two parts.

1. Pre-Offer
2. Offer Negotiation

1) PRE- OFFER

To effectively negotiate a job offer, it is very important to understand how talent teams and hiring managers go about determining offers. Let's start by discussing how job offers are created. Most companies have a formula or criteria they use to determine what the salary and compensation package will be. It is not a random number determined by someone in human resources; there is a process to it.

Companies will evaluate four key factors to determine an offer:

1. **Experience:** Your experience in the role is one key factor.

2. **Desired Compensation:** Employers will take into consideration the salary range the candidate is asking for in the process.

3. **Internal Equity (What the Position Pays):** Employers will most often have a salary range or "band" for each title and level. This is known as "internal equity" (or "pay equity"). It is used to prevent pay disparities and keep an equal pay culture. Often, a midpoint guides where the offer will be targeted. Typically, offers don't go to the very max or the very bottom. They tend to stay somewhere at or near the midpoint.

4. **Market Data:** Employers will often pay for compensation data and salary benchmarking tools from third-party sources to help determine salary ranges per position. For example, Radford data is a common tool employers use for salary benchmarking.

These four key factors are often used as a formula for determining what a suitable job offer should be for a potential new hire. Of course, compensation teams and internal human resources leaders will work with the hiring team to determine the final offer. However, each company has its own formula, which means it is not an exact science. My advice is to rely on your recruiter and ask good questions during the interview process to gain an understanding of expectations before you actually get to the offer stage.

What Are Salary History Ban Laws?

It is important to be aware of recent legislation on how companies communicate salary and compensation for job seekers. Salary history ban laws refer to legislative practices adopted mostly in the United States at the state level that ban employers from asking job seekers about their current or previous salaries. This basically means companies cannot ask what your current salary is, and you do not need to disclose it.

The purpose of these laws is to reduce the impact of historical discrimination and close the gender gap in pay. Keep in mind that not all states have adopted these laws. You can learn which have adopted salary history ban laws by doing a simple internet search. That said, it has become widely accepted that most companies will now refrain from asking job candidates what their salary history is.

How Can You Determine What Your Dream Job Pays?

Of course, all job seekers want to know what they can earn in their potential new dream job. It has recently become common practice for employers to now list the salary range in their job postings. This is because many states have now adopted **pay transparency laws.** Pay transparency legislation requires employers to disclose salary information to job candidates and current employees, making workplaces more transparent and equitable.

The important thing to keep in mind is that employers will often provide a very wide range, which is done on purpose. Please do not expect to be paid at the very high end of the range or the very low end. Providing a wide range is a way for companies to safeguard themselves, so set your expectations accordingly.

How Can You Determine the Salary Range for a Position If It Is Not Listed?

The easiest way to learn about salary and compensation is through your recruiter if you are working with one. They should be able to share all the compensation details with you and help you in the negotiation. If you are not working with a recruiter, you will need to ask this question during the interview. As I mentioned earlier, I do not recommend asking salary or compensation questions during the first interview. You will want to save that question for when you are further into the process.

Now, for smaller companies where there may not be a lot of interview rounds, you need to ask this question first: "How many steps are there in the interview process?" That way, you can determine when you will need to discuss compensation. Bringing up salary too early makes it sound like you're only about the money. Asking too late may mean you don't have the information you need to negotiate. So, this is very tricky.

Another way to learn about the compensation range for your dream job is to ask during an informational interview with a potential mentor. Be careful how you ask. You never want to ask someone what they are making. Instead, ask if they can give you an idea of what you might expect to make in the role based on your level of experience.

Mentors can also be a very good resource when it comes to salary advice. So, if you have a mentor, ask their opinion on this matter. That said, do not trust some random Joe Schmo who is offering advice. I would make sure you know and trust your source. Online salary tools and information can often be quite inaccurate, so they shouldn't be used as your only source.

How to Prepare Yourself for the Question, "What Are Your Salary Expectations?"

Perhaps the most dreaded interview question job candidates can get is: **"What are your salary expectations?"** Here are three tips on how to handle that question.

1. Try to avoid giving details. Do not blurt out numbers, even though that is what they are hoping for.

2. Try to defer this discussion to the very end of the process, if possible.

3. Name a range, not a number. Research conducted by psychologists at Columbia Business School found job applicants who named a range during salary negotiations received significantly higher overall salaries than those who offered a specific number. This approach proves particularly effective when the range's lower end aligns with the applicant's desired salary. Basically, the offer is probably going to come in at the low end of the range. Therefore, it is advisable to set the lowest number in the range at a level that you find acceptable. If the position is offered to you at that low range, you should be prepared to take it if that's what you gave them.

How Does a Recruiter Assist in the Job Offer Process?

Your recruiter should be a huge help before and during the job offer process. They should be able to share their experience and history with the client and company, which includes explaining the compensation range and details. Expect them to assist in all aspects of the offer and negotiation process. They should know what is negotiable and what is not. Good recruiters will act as your advisor and liaison between you and the company. They should also be able to tell you whether or not a job offer is "best and final" when it is presented. This is going to be very important to know. My advice is to rely on your recruiter and their expertise in this process.

2) OFFER NEGOTIATION

How Are Job Offers Typically Presented?

In most cases, job offers are presented verbally first. Companies want to assess interest level and get an idea of whether or not they can expect the candidate to accept the position before preparing the offer in writing. Written offers take a lot of work and often mean several signatures from higher-ups. There may also be a backup candidate for the position. So, if a verbal offer is presented and it is a no, they can quickly pivot to the other candidate.

Also, once a written offer goes out, it is much harder to retract. Written offers will most often be presented after a company gets a verbal "yes" from the candidate and will come in the form of a letter via email. In some cases, believe it or not, some companies still send letters via snail mail to your home address. What's most common right now is an offer letter in writing with some type of electronic signature required.

Who Typically Presents the Offers, and How Long Do You Have to Decide?

Offers are typically presented by one of three people: the hiring manager for the position, a human resources manager, or your recruiter. Please keep in mind that the person who presents the offer does not hold any weight in how much they want you for the position. Do not think that if your recruiter presents the offer to you, it is any less important than if the hiring manager presents it. It's simply just a matter of company preference. Most offers are presented via phone conversation, but you may get details via email first and then by phone. How you respond to these details is very important. We will discuss that later in this chapter.

A **job offer deadline** simply refers to when you need to provide an answer. The typical range is from 24 to 72 hours. Some offer letters may say up to one week. One week is not ideal or appreciated by employers, so I do not advise waiting that long to respond. Offer deadlines will vary from employer to employer.

In my opinion, 48 hours is a reasonable time for you to get back to an employer on a job offer. Some may think 48 hours is quick, but if you have been interviewing for weeks, sometimes even months, you should be able to know at that point whether or not you want to accept the job.

However, there may be reasons for needing more time. If you are still waiting on or negotiating details, it may require more time. That said, the longer it takes to decide on an offer, the worse the impression. Time is the death of all offers. There is such a thing as deal fatigue, meaning the longer an offer sits, the more clouded it becomes. It does not provide a great impression on your future employer. If an offer takes too long to develop and the decision is not made, it just looks like the candidate either doesn't want the position or is trying to buy time for another opportunity. I would be careful with how long it takes you to get back to the company with a decision.

10 Things to Consider During Job Offer Negotiations (Job Offer Negotiation Checklist)

It is extremely important to be well prepared in advance of the job offer negotiation process. Here are 10 important questions you should ask yourself before and during the job offer negotiation process so you can be prepared:

1. What is the range for the position? And what is the total compensation potential?
2. What do you currently earn? And what is your current total compensation?
3. What salary would it take for you to say yes?
4. What total compensation package are you hoping for?
5. What are you walking away from currently (bonuses, long-term incentives, stock payouts, etc.)?
6. When can you start?
7. How much notice do you need to give your current employer?

8. How long have you been on the job market?
9. How many other job prospects do you currently have in the works? Any potential offers in the works?
10. Any obstacles, planned vacations, or days needed off before or soon after you start?

The answers to these questions will help you decide what it would take for you to accept an offer. It will also prepare you for questions you will likely get from the company. Many of these questions will be asked of you. Your recruiter should know all of this information as well, so be sure to share these details in advance so they can help you in the job offer negotiation.

Communication Breakdown

One of the most common downfalls in the job search process is communication breakdown. We recently had a candidate complete a very lengthy and extensive job interview for her dream job. The odds were against her. Unfortunately, she was passed over for the position and was devastated! In addition to calling my recruiter who was working with her, she called me directly to share in her disappointment, begging me to help her win a position.

As luck would have it, the position with our client reopened, and she was selected. She literally screamed with excitement when learning of the offer. Soon after, this candidate completely disappeared. She was unresponsive for several days. We soon learned that when she shared the news with her husband, he was not supportive of her accepting the position. The job search process had been months in the making, with hours and hours of interactions, interviewing, preparation, planning, and process for her, us, and our client. The offer came in way higher than we had expected. She still turned it down. The missing and critical piece to this equation was that her husband was pursuing a position in a different city that would cause them to move.

How could this have possibly gone as far as it did without her having this conversation with her spouse ahead of time? It is extremely important to be as transparent as possible with those involved in your search. This includes your recruiter, the hiring team at the company, your spouse, your parents, or whoever needs to be involved in the final decision. Ask the right questions. Share critical information before, during, and after the process. This will prevent surprises and last-minute mishaps.

What Is the Best Strategy for Negotiating a Job Offer?

There are many ways to negotiate job offers. I will share three simple ways that I find most effective:

1. **Offer a range, not a number.** We discussed this in detail earlier in this chapter.

2. **Don't be desperate.** I know this sounds very obvious, but it's easier said than done. Throughout this book, I have explained the importance of showing interest, excitement, and enthusiasm. Now, I'm telling you not to be desperate. There is a fine line that you need to walk to do both. You want to make sure the company still respects your level of interest and excitement. However, you want them to feel that you *want* the job but don't *need* the job. There's a big difference.

3. **Find leverage.** Finding leverage is going to make it much easier for you to show that you want the job but don't need it. Here are two examples of how you can use leverage.

Leverage Example (Other Opportunities)

"In full transparency, I'm considering two opportunities with other companies, and those positions pay in a slightly higher range than this position. Please know that the opportunity at your company is still my top choice. I was just hoping the salary would just be a little higher and in the range of the other opportunities."

Leverage Example (Other Offer)

Perhaps the best way to use leverage is if you already have another offer in hand. If another company has presented you with an offer, you should use that as leverage because you have become more marketable. Everyone wants what they can't have. Everyone wants what everyone else wants. So, use that to your advantage. Your response may sound like this:

"In full transparency, I have received an offer from another organization. However, the opportunity at your company is still my top choice, so I really want to make this work and am hoping the salary can be increased to (name a number)."

These are the three best strategies that I have found for negotiating an offer. The most important thing I will say is, please just be tactful throughout the process. I would not advise leveraging other opportunities or offers unless they are real. I have seen people get caught exaggerating or fabricating other offers to help in their negotiations.

When Is It Beneficial to Disclose Your Current Salary?

During the job offer negotiation, it may be a competitive advantage to disclose your current salary to potentially drive their offer up. Employers know that no one wants to take a step back, so if your current compensation is higher, leverage it.

> **Caution:** If your salary is **much** higher than the top side of their range, I would not disclose it. You may actually price yourself out of the position if the company feels it is too large a pay cut and may potentially make you a flight risk.
>
> As an example, I am working with a job seeker who was recently downsized from a very senior-level position. His annual base salary was $250,000. This gentleman is 56 years old and only wants to work for another five to seven years. He understands that in the current market, he may not be able to find an employer to match or even come close to his prior salary. He is willing to accept compensation in the $175K range. However, a company would see this as a $75,000 pay cut. Most employers, if aware of this discrepancy, would consider this candidate a "flight risk." Therefore, it is better not to disclose his compensation to potential employers.

When to Avoid Disclosing Your Current Compensation

Do not disclose your salary if you are currently making less than the low side of the range or if you are not fully sure what the range is and where you stand in comparison. Sharing your salary if it is low may result in the company coming in with a number that is an increase for you but lower than where it may have been if they were not aware of what you are currently making. Also, if you are concerned about stereotypes and gender discrimination, it is best not to disclose your compensation. Keep in mind that salary history ban laws will protect you from having to do so.

How to Handle an Offer When It's Presented

It is very important to be mindful of your initial reaction and response to an offer. Again, it will likely be presented via phone, and the person presenting the details will be paying very close attention to your response. I recommend that your very first words are: "Thank you." What you say next will vary. You might say, "Thank you. I accept," or "Thank you. I'm truly grateful to receive this offer and will discuss it with my [family/spouse] so I can get back to you promptly with an answer."

The important thing is to never balk or show disappointment when an offer is presented. Companies are typically very excited to present you with an offer and want to see that enthusiasm matched. Even if the offer comes in lower than you expect, be gracious. Don't think that if you come off as thankful and show gratitude, it is going to prevent you from negotiating. That's not true. You can still negotiate; you just want to give them the right first impression. Be tactful and professional in all of your dialogue and interactions during the offer process. You never want to come off as ungrateful, sour grapes, or disappointed in any way.

Lastly, be responsive. If the company or your recruiter reaches out to you, respond within 24 hours. If you do not respond to requests for more information or a status check, it's going to appear as if you're trying to buy more time, you're indecisive, or you just don't want the job. I would hate to see that happen. Remember, this is your potential future employer. You do not want to start your new job on a bad note.

Is It True You Should Never Accept an Initial Offer?

According to Fidelity Investments, 85% of Americans and 87% of professionals ages 25 to 35 who countered on salary, other compensation, benefits, or both pay and other compensation and benefits got at least some of what they asked for.

> **Caution:** I do not always recommend negotiating an initial offer just for the sake of doing so, because of the statistics I just shared or because someone told you to. Never negotiate the initial offer if you have already been informed that the offer being presented is "best and final." Best and final means their best and final offer. Also, if the offer came in exactly where you expected it to and it was what you asked for, accept it! Start the celebration and get ready to start your new career. You deserve it!

Do Not Over-Negotiate

Know when to stop asking and when to stop holding out. Remember, you need to be tactful and professional at all times. Do not push too hard. Too many times, I've seen this turn the whole deal south. You can talk yourself right out of the job if you are not careful.

Let me share a story with you about Jim Haines. Jim was a job seeker we were working with who received an offer that came in exactly where we expected, and it was exactly what he had asked for. To my surprise, I received an irate phone call from my client telling me that when they presented the offer to Jim, he balked. He appeared disappointed and wanted to negotiate.

When speaking to Jim, I found out that his wife, who is a financial professional of some sort, had prompted him to negotiate for more money. This "after the fact" negotiation tactic upset everyone in the process. Unfortunately, it upset the company so much that they rescinded the offer. Jim called me, devastated, and asked me if I could fix it. Unfortunately, after several attempts, not only would the company not reconsider the offer, but they actually refused to do business with us again. The company actually blamed us for Jim taking this negotiation tactic even though we had no knowledge of it. We explained it wasn't our idea and came from Jim's wife. It just didn't matter. At that point, everyone lost.

Why Is It a Good Idea to Accept an Initial Offer?

Accepting an initial offer makes a great impression. It starts things off on a solid note with your new employer. Many offers come in better than expected, so move forward and don't complicate things. Too many times, I've seen things go bad when candidates negotiate an initial offer just for the sake of doing so. Make no mistake. If the offer is not where you want it to be, you can certainly negotiate it as long as you follow the steps I mentioned above. There is no better feeling than reaching the finish line, getting a great offer, and celebrating the success of winning your dream job.

YOU ARE NEXT!

START CALLOUT BOX

Free Download: Job Offer Negotiation Checklist.

Scan the QR code:

Chapter 11 Summary

Negotiate Your Way to Success

- Pre-Offer
    - Four Key Factors That Determine an Offer
    - What Are Salary History Ban Laws?
    - How Can You Determine What Your Dream Job Pays?
    - Pay Transparency Laws
    - How Can You Determine the Salary Range for a Position If It Is Not Listed?
    - How to Prepare Yourself for the Question, "What Are Your Salary Expectations?"
    - How Does a Recruiter Assist in the Job Offer Process?
- Offer Negotiation
    - How Are Job Offers Typically Presented?
    - Who Typically Presents the Offers, and How Long Do You Have to Decide?
    - The Job Offer Deadline
    - Job Offer Negotiation Checklist (10 Things to Consider)
    - Communication Breakdown
    - What Is the Best Strategy for Negotiating a Job Offer?
    - Leverage Example (Other Opportunities)
    - Leverage Example (Other Offer)
    - When Is It Beneficial to Disclose Your Current Salary?
    - When to Avoid Disclosing Your Current Compensation
    - How to Handle an Offer When It's Presented
    - Is It True You Should Never Accept an Initial Offer?
    - Do Not Over-Negotiate
    - Why Is It a Good Idea to Accept an Initial Offer?

CHAPTER 12

The System

I spoke to a job seeker this week who was in desperate need of guidance. She explained that it had been exactly one year since she'd been part of a massive layoff at her former company, and she shared some statistics from her unsuccessful 12-month job search:

- Over four hundred applications.
- Over 50 interviews.
- Several three-to-five-week gaps in communication between rounds of interviews.
- Several no-shows at scheduled interview times (often with little or no explanation).
- Several "final" interviews where it came down to her and another candidate. Here are some of the results of those final interviews:
  - We decided to go with a different candidate."
  - "After further consideration, we feel you are overqualified for the role."
  - "The position has been put on hold due to budget constraints."
  - "The position was eliminated and will no longer be filled."

I do NOT want this to be you. The entire purpose of this book is to give you guidance and an advantage over other job seekers. For that to happen, we need to put all this together and start executing the plan. The way to do that is to be disciplined and consistent with the SYSTEM.

The SYSTEM is to schedule time in your calendar each day to include the daily job search actions we discussed throughout this book. If you are currently employed, this could mean finding a chunk of time in the morning, a chunk of time at lunch, and a chunk of time in the evening. If you are not currently working, your "day job" should now be your job search. You should consider spending as much time as you can each day to work on this process.

The key is to strategically and systematically plan your days to include job search actions. Remember the Charles Barkley story? The NBA Hall of Famer did not lose 50+ pounds all at once. He did it 10 pounds at a time. The same goes for you and your job search. Break it off into manageable increments and chunks of time.

Let's review some of the key job search actions we discussed in this book and come up with some examples of chunking time.

Daily Job Search Actions

- Research Job Openings (30 Minutes per day).
- Send Out LinkedIn Connection Invites (15 per Day).
- Send Out LinkedIn Networking Messages (Five per Day).
- LinkedIn Engagement (10 to 15 Minutes per Day).
- Content Creation and Posting (15 Minutes, Four Times per Week).
- Optimize and Prepare Resume for Specific Job Applications (30 Minutes per Day).
- Seek Employee Referrals for New Positions (One Hour per Week).
- Interact With and Reach Out to Recruiters (30 Minutes per Week).
- Complete Informational Interviews (Two per Week, 60 Minutes).
- Practice Interviewing (One to Two Hours per Week).

- Follow-Ups (10 Minutes, Two Times per Week).
- Celebrate Small Wins (Daily).

Let me explain this in a different way. **If you were to...**

- Save $8 per day—you would have $3,000 at the end of the year.
- Read 20 pages per day—would equal approximately 30 books per year.
- Walk 10,000 steps each day—would equate to 70 marathons in a year.
- Systematically complete your well-defined job search actions = **WIN your dream job!**

This book is *Job Search Mastery: How to WIN Your Dream Job* because you need to do just that: you need to WIN the job. I do not believe that people just land a job. People win jobs. Do not underestimate the cumulative effect of committing to small daily actions.

What I need you to do now is develop your system. What job search actions will you schedule each day? What are your job search action goals for the week? What will you accumulate by the end of the month? Ask yourself these questions and develop your plans each week so you can achieve the progress you deserve.

Consistency Is KEY

Our potential is unlimited, but our time is not. TAKE ACTION! Timing is a factor. The key to your job search success is discipline and consistency. When you are disciplined and consistent in your daily actions, you will see progress, and things will come together. You will start to pile up small wins. The small wins will result in bigger outcomes. Taking consistent action will create habits that will compound to build your career identity. Without realizing it, you will amass assets in the form of a high-converting resume, a kick-ass LinkedIn profile, interview experience and success, strong relationships, a vast network of professionals in your dream job community, a strong personal and professional brand with great engagement, negotiation skills, and the ability to do it all over again if needed.

And YES, you will WIN your dream job.

You will establish yourself in an amazing career.

You will realize the vision you set out for.

You will WIN!

Free Download: Daily Job Search Action Planner.

Scan the QR code:

Chapter 12 Summary

THE SYSTEM

- What Is THE SYSTEM?
- **Consistency Is KEY**
- **Commit to Daily Job Search Actions**
- **Research Job Openings (30 Minutes per Day).**
- **Send Out LinkedIn Connection Invites (15 per Day)**
- **Send Out LinkedIn Networking Messages (Five Per Day)**
- **LinkedIn Engagement (10 Minutes per Day)**

- Content Creation and Posting (15 Minutes, Four Times per Week)
- Optimize and Prepare Resume for Specific Job Applications (30 Minutes per Day)
- Seek Job Referrals for New Positions (Two Hours per Week)
- Interact With and Reach Out to Recruiters (30 Minutes per Week)
- Complete Informational Interviews (Two per Week, 60 Minutes)
- Practice Interviewing (One to Two Hours per Week)
- Follow-Ups (10 Minutes, Two Times per Week)
- Celebrate Small Wins (Daily)

Conclusion

You now have everything you need to secure your dream job. You know the system. You know the process. I promised to walk you through the steps and provide a resource with my experience, knowledge, advice, tips, tricks, and best practices in one place. Now, it is up to you to implement everything.

The reality is that many of you reading this may not implement any of it. You read it and maybe got some pointers, but will you really execute on this? Will you follow each step? Will you commit to the daily actions required to achieve progress and pile up wins? Or will you stay on the sidelines, watching others play the game?

You may have noticed the common trend that certain gyms offer memberships for $10 to $20 per month. How can they afford to do that when most gyms charge $50 to $60 per month? Because according to data from Exercise.com, 67% of the people who join gyms, even the more expensive ones, never show up. (A small percentage of people will be consistent. A small percentage of people will actually implement and execute each day, each week, and each month. What will you do? Will you show up for yourself now that you have the system that can bring you success?

In Chapter 1, you learned that job search success starts in your mind. Prepare yourself mentally for the fact that success will not happen overnight. This is normal; it is not just you. Instead, seek progress over perfection. Be obsessed and view your job search as a contest, a competition, because it is. Failure will be inevitable, so embrace it. Learn from it and pivot forward in the 24 hours after a rejection. If you get stuck or start to feel frustrated or overwhelmed, just get back to the process and stop worrying about the outcome. Most important, be disciplined and work the system.

Success is earned and requires consistent effort. Please know that this is an investment in yourself and your future. I recently heard Alex Hermozi (entrepreneur, best-selling author, and investor) say, "The outcome isn't the thing you are building. The person *you are* is the thing you are building. It's about who we become while we are doing the work, more than the outcome itself."

Do the work, put in the effort each day, and you will build a career you never imagined.

Remember, I believe in you. I think it is only fitting to end this book the way we started. I believe in you now more than ever. Why? Because YOU are still reading this, which shows me that you finish what you start. YOU keep the promises you make to yourself and are part of the TOP percentile. YOU are truly committed to investing in yourself and your career. You've also made it further than many others who only read a few chapters or perhaps never read any of this at all.

But YOU…

You WILL find the discipline.

You WILL be consistent with your daily actions.

You WILL be systematic each day.

You WILL WIN your dream job!

Congratulations… YOU are now a *Job Search Master*!

INVITATION

Let's Stay Connected

I invite you to stay connected with me through social media. I would love to learn about your progress and see YOU win your dream job. I want to be there to congratulate you and celebrate your success.

I can be found on several platforms. Scan the QR Code below:

I am hoping I can continue this journey with you, and I invite you to keep in touch. I promise to share more tips, tricks, advice, and encouragement. I promise to commit myself to sharing the very best of what I learn in hopes that it can help thrust you into new levels of your career, personal growth, and future success.

~ ALL THE BEST,
Tom

Acknowledgments

This book would not have been possible without the tremendous support system I have in my family, friends, co-workers, coaches, clients, colleagues, and, of course, all of YOU, the job seekers who motivate me to be better in my career. YOU motivated me to write this book in hopes that it would be a guide and resource that will bring dream jobs to all who read it.

Special Thanks to:

- First and foremost, I want to thank GOD! I am grateful for this path, this passion, this promise. Thank YOU for taking me places I could have never gone on my own.

- My wife, Kris: who motivates and encourages me EVERY day to stretch the boundaries of what I think is possible.

- My daughter, Ava: a brilliant mind who has shown me what true resilience, grit, and hard work look like while maintaining a HUGE heart.

- My son, Dean: a true leader, who has shown me bravery and what it means to take the road less traveled by doing what few people would choose to do.

- My mom: who taught me confidence, hard work, and the importance of staying true to what I know I am capable of.

- My dad: who exemplified what it means to be a man of integrity, kindness, quiet leadership, and consistency.

- My brother, Joe, and sister, Stephanie: who willingly dedicated more hours of inspiration and support over all these years than you will ever know. Thank you for being in my corner.

- Uncle Ralph: a true role model, leader, and inspiration who set the standard for what I could become while always encouraging the expansion of my mind and the pursuit of my dreams.

- Craig: wish you were here. I know you would be proud.

- ALL my family… aunts, uncles, cousins, "fousins," in-laws, out-laws, nieces, nephews (first, second, twice removed). You know who you are, and I am grateful for each and every one of you.

- ALL my friends, too many to mention, but you all know who you are. LOVE you guys and appreciate every second that we get to do what we do. Ok, Bart, I will mention you by name, so you've made it into my book.

- My teammates at The Carolan Group, who exemplify our company core values (positivity, intention, transparency, integrity, trust, and excellence) each day, show me true loyalty and commitment, and motivate me to be better personally as well as professionally. I am truly grateful and honored that I get to go to battle with you each day.

- My coaches and mentors, for your inspiration, guidance, tough love, and, most importantly, for setting the standard and holding me accountable to it. Ed Mylett, Andy Frisella, and all the leaders and friends in the Arete Syndicate. Ben Newman and the Uncommon Live Community. Donnie Gupton, Gary Stauble, and all my colleagues in the recruiting industry.

- My podcast community and listeners all over the world. You have a huge place in my heart, my life, and my mission. Thank you for your support.

THANK YOU FOR READING MY BOOK!

I appreciate your interest in my book and value your feedback as it helps me improve future versions of this book.

I would appreciate it if you could leave your invaluable review on Amazon.com with your feedback. Thank you!

www.ingramcontent.com/pod-product-compliance
Lightning Source LLC
Chambersburg PA
CBHW060134100426
42744CB00007B/778